The Courage Way

Leading And Living With Integrity

Center For Courage & Renewal And Shelly L. Francis

Foreword By Parker J. Palmer
Author Of Let Your Life Speak

16pt

Read How You Want
LARGE PRINT BOOKS, BRAILLE & DAISY

Copyright Page from the Original Book

The Courage Way

Berrett-Koehler Publishers, Inc.
1333 Broadway, Suite 1000
Oakland, CA 94612-1921
Tel: (510) 817-2277, Fax: (510) 817-2278
www.bkconnection.com

Excerpt from "An Away-Day with the Shadow" from *E-mail from the Soul: New and
Selected Leadership Poems* by William Ayot. Copyright 2014. Used by permission of
William Ayot.
"Relay" from *The Art and Spirit of Leadership* by Judy Brown. Copyright 2012. Used
by permission of Judy Brown.
Excerpt from "Potbound" written in 1990 and used by permission of Diana Chapman
Walsh.
Excerpts from "Where I'm From" written in 2017 and used by permission of Susan M.
Glisson and Charles H. Tucker.

Ordering information for print editions
Quantity sales. Special discounts are available on quantity purchases by corporations,
associations, and others. For details, contact the "Special Sales Department" at the
Berrett-Koehler address above.
Individual sales. Berrett-Koehler publications are available through most bookstores.
They can also be ordered directly from Berrett-Koehler: Tel: (800) 929-2929; Fax:
(802) 864-7626; www.bkconnection.com
Orders for college textbook/course adoption use. Please contact Berrett-Koehler:
Tel: (800) 929-2929; Fax: (802) 864-7626.
Orders by U.S. trade bookstores and wholesalers. Please contact Ingram Publisher
Services, Tel: (800) 509-4887; Fax: (800) 838-1149; E-mail: customer
.service@ingrampublisherservices.com; or visit www.ingrampublisherservices.com/
Ordering for details about electronic ordering.

First Edition
Hardcover print edition ISBN 978-1-62656-775-7
PDF e-book ISBN 978-1-62656-776-4
IDPF e-book ISBN 978-1-62656-777-1

2017-1

Production manager: Susan Geraghty. Cover design: Paula Goldstein. Interior design
and composition: Andrea Reider. Copyeditor: Michele D. Jones. Proofreader: Sophia
Ho. Indexer: Sylvia Coates. Author photo: Fat Yeti Photography.

TABLE OF CONTENTS

Praise for The Courage Way   i

Foreword: Parker J. Palmer   viii

Preface: A Word from the Voice Between the Lines xvii

Introduction: Why Courage?   xxvii

1: What Is the Courage Way?   1

2: The Inner Work of Leadership   33

3: Have You Met Your True Self?   59

4: Courage Takes Trust   83

5: Reflection in Community   109

6: The Courage to Care for True Self   130

7: The Courage to Answer Your Calling   150

8: The Courage to Question and Listen   171

9: The Courage to Hold Tension in Life-Giving Ways 197

10: The Courage to Choose Wisely   219

11: The Courage to Connect and Trust in Each Other   239

12: The Courage to Stay or to Leave   266

Notes   289

Quote Sources   309

Recommended Reading   320

Gratitudes   322

About the Coauthor   328

Index   335

Praise for The Courage Way

"At a time when civil discourse reflects a lack of trust in leadership and when the integrity of our leaders seems in doubt, Shelly Francis offers us a path to renewal. Her insights into cultivating courage through daily practice provide a much-needed guide to authentic leadership aimed at prosperity and flourishing. Essential reading in today's world!"
—**Chris Laszlo, PhD, Char and Chuck Fowler Professor of Business as an Agent of World Benefit, Department of Organizational Behavior, Weatherhead School of Management; Faculty Executive Director, The Fowler Center, Case Western Reserve University; and coauthor (with Judy Sorum Brown) of *Flourishing Enterprise***

"Leading with integrity and empathy requires vision and a connection to your deepest self. Yet leading people and businesses also requires immense effort

and dedication that can isolate you, exhaust you, and even pull you away from your vision and deep connection. Enter *The Courage Way,* which offers tools, stories, and ideas to help you cultivate your vision and your ability to lead with courage, kindness, humor, and dignity. Shelly Francis illuminates the work of Parker J. Palmer with wit and grace."
—Karla McLaren, MEd, author of
***The Language of Emotions* and**
The Art of Empathy

"In this troubled world today, we need to check our moral preferences as leaders and commit to what we value and will defend. In healthcare, I have learned that the secret to quality is love. It is also justice, which is the manifestation of love in our public policies and conduct. *The Courage Way* offers stories and practices of how the hearts of leaders can stay connected with their moral compass and courage. It shows that what we create collectively arises from the wholeness and compassion we locate within."

—**Donald M. Berwick, MD, President Emeritus and Senior Fellow, Institute for Healthcare Improvement and former Administrator, Centers for Medicare and Medicaid Services**

"*The Courage Way* will nourish that part of you that cares deeply about the world. A soulful approach for helping you harness your inner strength to become the kind of leader the world needs now—in every dimension of your life."
—**Jono Fisher, founder of** WakeUpProject.com

"Everyone should read this gem of a book. *The Courage Way* is a powerful tonic for our challenging times. Keep it close at hand so you can savor its life-giving music again and again."
—**Dr. Gloria J. Burgess, distinguished scholar, professor of transformational leadership, and author of *Dare to Wear Your Soul on the Outside, Pass It On!,* and *Flawless Leadership***

"*The Courage Way* forever expands the way we think about courage, bringing its many manifestations to life and proving that acts of courage, whether physical, moral, creative, or otherwise, have their seeds within each and every one of us. The poignant stories that Shelly Francis shares make the heroic qualities of courage more understandable and accessible than ever before. This would be an important book at any time, but at this moment, when America is divided and hurting, it illuminates the courage within that promises a way through. Read and re-energize!"
—Billy Shore, founder and CEO, Share Our Strength, and author of *The Cathedral Within* and *The Imaginations of Unreasonable Men*

"This is an important read for leaders at all levels. I am inspired by the promise and potential of leaders and organizations as forces for good, and this has never been more important in the world. *The Courage Way* shares time-tested tools, reflections, and guiding principles that every leader can

learn and practice. This can move leaders and their organizations toward flourishing through creating human-centered cultures guided by strong ethics and integrity."
—Richard J. Davidson, founder of the Center for Healthy Minds, University of Wisconsin–Madison, and coauthor (with Daniel Goleman) of *Altered Traits*

"*The Courage Way* by Shelly Francis is a wonderfully written book for all those who wish to lead their personal and professional lives in alignment with what truly matters. Happiness is unthinkable without courage, yet until now, little has been written about how to muster this great virtue. The book is a must-have resource—inspiring!"
—Andrea F. Polard, PsyD, founder of Zen Psychology Therapy and author of *A Unified Theory of Happiness*

"What would you do with more courage? From that first provocative question to the last story of people learning to lead and live in deeper

alignment with themselves, *The Courage Way* is a surprising and counterintuitive remedy for the heart-sore. My calling is to sit with those whose hearts have been broken open by their calling, by their deep desire to live life in synchronicity with their truest values, beliefs, wishes, and dreams. *The Courage Way* offers a way to do that gently, yet it fiercely offers ways forward. Shelly Francis and the Center for Courage & Renewal have again demonstrated their ability to lead each of us into a new way of being."
—Jerry Colonna, Cofounder and CEO, Reboot.io

*For the Courage Collaboration,
thank you for your voices and your
 courage on the ground.*

*For Wil and Rus, Grace and J.J.,
may you always bring your true self to
 your life's work.*

Foreword

Parker J. Palmer

In the early 1990s, with the generous support of the Fetzer Institute, I planted the seeds of what would eventually become the Center for Courage & Renewal—seeds that grew rapidly under the wise, visionary, and grounded leadership of my friends, colleagues, and cofounders, Marcy Jackson and Rick Jackson.

The idea behind our work is to help leaders show up more fully in the workplace—and in every dimension of their lives—with their identity and integrity in hand and intact. To put it another way, we help leaders "rejoin soul and role" in order to gain transformative leverage on the work they do, the institutions in which they do it, and the larger world. As the great social movements have demonstrated, the human soul—or identity and integrity—is an Archimedean point of leverage from which people have moved the world, whether or not they are "positional" leaders.

When I planted those early seeds with the help of the Fetzer Institute, I had no idea that by 2018, they would grow into

- Three hundred well-trained facilitators in the United States, Australasia, Canada, Latin America, the United Kingdom, and Spain, with allied work in South Korea
- Thousands of Courage & Renewal programs of many descriptions
- Tens of thousands of leaders in a range of professions whose lives and work have been transformed by those programs
- Hundreds of thousands of individuals and institutions who've benefited from those transformed leaders

Nor did I ever imagine that someday there would be a book called *The Courage Way* written by Shelly Francis, my good friend and very able colleague for the past five years. As the Center's marketing and communications director, Shelly has been our chief "story collector," helping us understand what we do, reminding us why we do it, and sharing our story with others.

No one is better equipped than Shelly to write about the components of the Courage Way and to illustrate how transformative they can be, using stories of some of the leaders who've been changed by Courage Work. The book you're holding in your hands is evidence aplenty to back that claim.

I published my first book in 1980. From that day forward, I've been committed to "putting wheels" on my ideas. I did not want to put words on the page and let them lie there passively hoping that someone would read them and, in a few cases, apply them. I wanted to create vehicles with those words—vehicles such as workshops, retreats, and other programs that people could use in pursuit of personal and communal ends, drawing on their own inner resources and the support of a community of peers.

Thanks to hundreds of colleagues and supporters, that's exactly what we've been able to do over the past quarter century—not only with my ideas but with the ideas of many others who have joined in and contributed to the Courage & Renewal cause.

Leaders in many fields—education, health care, business, nonprofit, philanthropy, and religion—have been nurtured by the ideas and practices embedded in Courage Work. It takes courage to "join soul and role" in organizations that make it unsafe to show up with integrity and act in alignment with it. But when we find that courage, our lives become more whole, our work reaches deeper, the people we serve are better served, and, in ways large and small, the world becomes a better place.

As you will learn from this book, Courage Work takes many forms, depending on the setting. But whatever the form, it is rooted in the principles and practices of what we call a Circle of Trust—a way of creating the conditions where people can do inner work in community. The components that go into creating those conditions—the components Shelly has so deftly named and explained in this book—have a proven capacity to touch and transform leaders and the work they do.

When I'm asked for an "elevator" example, the story that most often comes to mind involves a circle that I facilitated some years ago, composed of twenty-four physician leaders of medical residency programs.

During a large-group discussion of a poem about fidelity to purpose, one of the participants said, "I work in a health care system that has me on the edge of violating my Hippocratic Oath several times a week."

One component of Courage Work is deep listening, so no one jumped to respond to this man's comment. Instead, people made silent space for him to listen more deeply to himself. Out of that silence, this physician leader spoke a second time: "You know, that's the first time I've ever said that to a group of professional peers."

There was more silence, then this man spoke again, now in a quieter and more somber voice: "The truth is, that's the first time I've ever said it to myself."

When I heard those words, I knew I had witnessed a pivotal moment in one leader's personal and professional life. He had heard a truth from within that he could not argue with or push away, the way he might have if some "systems expert" had critiqued his workplace. The critique he heard came from his "inner teacher," and it put him on the horns of a dilemma: *Do I try to sweep under the rug what I just heard myself say, as if I'd never heard it? Or do I take that inner voice seriously and try to transform my workplace into one that supports rather than threatens my Hippocratic Oath?*

The Courage Work this physician did helped him find his courage as a leader. He returned to his job, identified colleagues who shared his concern, and, working together over a period of months, they were able to establish a penalty-free zone for the reporting of medical errors—a major systemic step toward helping hospitals "do no harm."

I hope that this story gives you a glimpse of what I mean when I say that Courage Work touches not only leaders but also their workplaces and the people they serve. Because of this book, you need not attend a Courage & Renewal event to be touched this way. Shelly has done a masterful job of extracting the principles and practices on which our programs are based, and of showing—via well-framed ideas and vivid stories of real people in a variety of leadership roles—how they have been and can be applied by individuals and groups in workaday life.

A final thought before I get out of the way and let Shelly carry on. One of the most important notions we deal with in Courage Work is this: no matter how much devotion and courage leaders bring to important tasks, their jobs are never done. We will forever stand in "the tragic gap," the gap between the hard realities around us and what we know to be possible because we see it with our own eyes from time to time.

Part of the Courage Way is learning to stand and act in that gap—which means resisting our ingrained cultural conviction that we must be "effective" if we and our work are to count for anything, that "Winning isn't everything; it's the *only* thing!"

We all want our work to be effective, of course. That's why we put so much time and energy into it. But if effectiveness is our only norm, we will die in despair, or drop out long before we have made our fullest contribution. Think of anyone you regard as courageous because he or she lived a life devoted to high values like love, truth, and justice. Now ask yourself whether he or she was able to die saying, "I'm sure glad I took on that task, because now everyone in the world can scratch it off their to-do list forever." The answer is obvious.

In order to continue working on vital tasks that will never be accomplished, we need a norm that does not replace but supersedes "effectiveness." The name of that norm, I think, is "faithfulness." Faithfulness to our own best gifts, faithfulness to the needs around us, and faithfulness to those points where our gifts might contribute to meeting some of those needs: that should be the ultimate measure of work well done and a life well lived.

It takes courage for leaders to persevere, to stand and act in the tragic gap, taking small steps day in and day out to create and sustain organizations where trust, integrity, and authenticity can flourish. If we are to make this world a better place, we need a lot of leaders who are willing and able to walk this way for the long haul.

Welcome to a book that offers guidance, inspiration, and practical support for people like that—for people like you.

Preface

A Word from the Voice Between the Lines

My job is to keep the meaning completely embodied in the work itself, and therefore alive and capable of change. I think that's how an artist can best speak as a member of a moral community: clearly, yet leaving around her words that area of silence, that empty space, in which other and further truths and perceptions can form in other minds.
—Ursula K. Le Guin

If you found this book, it also found you. What in your life right now resonates with the idea of courage and leading a life of integrity?

This book found me, too, by way of two other books. The first was *Let Your Life Speak.* The leader of a women's writing group I was in introduced me to this book by Parker J. Palmer around

2002. His words "self-care is never a selfish act" helped me overcome cancer-caregiver burnout. Ten years later, the same writing teacher and friend let me know of a job opening at the nonprofit Parker founded, called the Center for Courage & Renewal, which she saw on his Facebook page. I landed the job!

A couple years later, I was in a used bookstore when a yellowed paperback copy of *The Courage to Create* by Rollo May jumped off the shelf. "How can we acquire creative courage?" says a line on the cover. I say that creativity is my caffeine, but also that creativity once saved my life. Seeing that word paired with courage, I had to take the book home. My inner artist was hungry.

I say that this book now in your hands also found me, because I am the person who raised her hand to compose something that would take on a life of its own.

At first this book project was an outgrowth of our organization's endeavor to evolve its own purpose. What is our theory of change? How have we equipped, inspired, and sustained leaders for these challenging times? Are they better able to find meaning in their work by reconnecting who they are with what they do? Does that inner strength help them deliver a service or product that will make a difference for their organizations, their employees, and the customers or clients they serve? We sensed a ripple effect from stories folks told us, even though we know we provide only some ingredients in the complex mix of why and how people access their courage to lead. We wanted to dig further.

So I set off to gain insight through interviewing a broad range of people who have participated in our programs to see how they are applying Courage & Renewal ideas to their lives and leadership. In one-hour interviews with more than 120 people, one-on-one and sometimes in groups, I asked about Courage principles and practices they still use. I asked what was hard, what was different, what was better.

My job was to stitch together their stories with the underlying wisdom of Parker Palmer spanning his nine books, plus twenty-five years of our applied learning with leaders. I now know Parker not only as an author but also as a colleague and friend. I know him and love him as a regular guy and a wise elder. It was an honor to meet people who have experienced and now embody the ideas he writes about. It was daunting to decide how best to paint the whole picture.

During the writing process, as director of marketing and communications for the Center, I've also been testing these practices in my day job and inside my head, heart, and life. I had many "case study" hard days. The backdrop of book-making over three years included the natural life-span changes in our nonprofit organization: a retirement and a search for an executive director, almost a full turnover in both staff and board, and nearly doubling the size of our facilitator network. Add to that the elections of national leaders, polarized politics, ongoing wars, desperate refugees, the opioid epidemic, homelessness, too many shootings, too many suicides, natural disasters, manmade disasters, and two record-rainfall winters here in Seattle. All became metaphors and living proof that the world needs more courage everywhere every day. I've been paying attention 24/7 to how our practices can give me—and others—more courage and trust in life and at work.

Even though one of our touchstones says "Speak your truth using 'I' statements," I've aimed to stay mostly out of view in this book. It's not my leadership memoir. It's not the story of how the Center itself has grown or changed as an organization. Yet our learnings are here—informed by the voices of authentic leaders.

We're not here to insist that you must attend our Courage & Renewal programs, although you are welcome. We make no promise that your life will be changed by the time you read the last page. This book contains ideas to consider and stories of others further along on the path. Consider it a mix tape, a playlist, a snapshot in time. Consider it an invitation to more conversation. Consider my voice your companion.

Ideas are just words on the page until people bring them to life. It takes courage to create a meaningful life of integrity. It also requires good company. And practice. And space to ponder questions like this:

What would you do with more courage?

It takes courage
to teach
to lead
to serve
to heal
to speak up
to stand out
to look inward
to right wrongs.

It takes courage
to walk your talk
to stand your ground
to make waves
to ride waves
to find wholehearted ways
to be known as vulnerable
to love after loss
to love, period.

It takes courage
to say "I was wrong"
to say "I don't know"
to say "Let's find out"
to take enough time
to seek better answers instead of
quick fixes
to give yourself fully
to try making a difference

when the outcome is not
guaranteed.

It takes courage
to choose wisely and well
to go against the grain
to go into the wind
to point your boat
toward your true north
to lead others forward
to have faith in the future
and be fully present today.

It takes courage
to trust in the process
to be part of the process
to process your parts that are
shadows
to embrace your shadows as part
of your self
to also embrace your beauty and
light.

It takes courage
to know yourself well enough
to choose where your energy
comes from and goes
to trust it's possible
to trust what courage can do

and give yourself time to find out.

It takes courage
to give yourself time to renew
to give yourself over to grief
to give silence a chair at the table
to give doubt a chance to
show other options
to give the world your best self
and ideas
without giving up on your soul.

It takes courage to
be your whole self
so you can
do your best work
so you can
be the change you want to see
so you can
do what your worthy cause most
needs you to do.

It takes courage
to ask "*How* shall I be"
so that I can do [what?]
so the world can be
better
for all.

Leadership takes courage
and gives courage, too.

And courage takes trust.

—SHELLY L. FRANCIS

Introduction

Why Courage?

> To live into the future means to leap into the unknown, and this requires a degree of courage for which there is no immediate precedent and which few people realize.
>
> —Rollo May

Sigrid Wright didn't put on her seatbelt because she was moving her car only a short distance. It was December nineteenth, and she had parked her car next to the office to unload supplies for the company holiday party. The Community Environmental Council's office was on an old dairy farm and sat on a point on the Santa Barbara mesa, overlooking the valley.

It was an unusually warm and bright sunny day, even for California, and Sigrid was thinking about the press conference she was hosting that morning. As she was backing down the narrow winding driveway, her car got stuck on a bush. What happened next isn't entirely clear. She pumped the gas pedal a couple of times to get unstuck, and the car suddenly popped off the bushes and spun into a backward fishtail at a high speed over the cliff.

Sigrid's car flipped over dense chaparral and poison oak, rolling 120 feet until it landed upside down in a tree. It was the only tree on the hillside big enough to have stopped the car from tumbling another hundred feet. She was stunned, still alert in a pile of glass and blood on the inside roof of her car. She honked to alert her coworkers, hoping someone would hear and call 911. "Through courage, I guess, and probably grace too, I managed to stay conscious despite the severe head trauma."

The car was still running, so Sigrid opened the electric window and fell out the window. She then fell out of the tree, landing in poison oak. Sigrid started climbing uphill. "The EMTs and fire crews had to chainsaw their way down and really find their way to get to me."

That was in 2003. It took Sigrid many months and more courage to recover. Five years later, the 2008 stock market crash and recession called for a different kind of courage. Sigrid and her husband had to short-sell their house to stay financially afloat. Meanwhile, the Community Environmental Council's endowment shrank in half. In addition, as assistant director and one of the few staff members remaining after a massive multiyear transformation resulted in a new strategic direction for CEC, Sigrid was unclear about her growth path with the organization. Perhaps best known for hosting one of the very first Earth Day festivals in America in 1970, but since then as a "think-and-do tank," CEC has focused on deeply analyzing tough environmental problems and then applying creative, real-world solutions. That "think and do" style describes Sigrid's leadership, too.

For fifteen years, Sigrid had been in charge of the annual Earth Day festival, one of the biggest in the country. But the event was not integrated into the rest of organization's mission and received very little support. She wondered if it was time to just let it fold or to find a new way to rejuvenate it. Sigrid was feeling very stuck and unsure that her effort was going to pay off.

"We had a complete turnover in our board during that time. We also had a leadership transition in management. By the time we hit 2008, I was ready, *internally ready,* for great leadership, but it was unclear what form that would take."

"While I had some really great things in my life, collectively much in my world felt stuck or broken. I couldn't quite visualize how to move forward. The rather melodramatic image I had during that time was my thumb hovering over the red button. Like 'I'm going to just blow this up. I'm out! I'm out!' I probably wasn't the only person after the great recession to consider making a dramatic change: new job, new town, new life."

"It took an enormous amount of grit and courage to just keep showing up. And to move incrementally to untangle piece by piece of what felt like a

Gordian knot that I was not going to get undone. Often I think of courage as those moments of what it takes to just scrap your way heroically, and the levels of determination we're capable of when we're fighting for our lives. But it actually took a lot more grit to just stay and move more incrementally, and work with what you have."

Around then, Sigrid joined the first cohort of a program created precisely because of the recession to help local nonprofit leaders keep going without losing heart.[1] An opportunity for renewal and reflection along with peer support was just what she needed. "It caught me at the right time and kept me from leaving the nonprofit sector. I don't know what I would have done other than this. I was not designed for government or the for-profit sector. I was really designed for nonprofit work."

Sigrid had thought that courage would be more a matter of daring, of taking a risk to leave CEC or Santa Barbara, but ultimately she came to believe that for her, on a personal level, courage was being willing to stick through the hard times.

A World Calling for Courage

Sometimes leadership feels as though you've driven backwards off a cliff (or have been pushed) and you have to crawl your way back to the top, broken and bruised. Sometimes we balance precariously on the edge of burnout. It takes courage to lead in the face of so many challenges. "Staying conscious" during Sigrid's rescue and return to health became her metaphor for leadership in the years right after 2008. But the stress for leaders now, a decade later, cannot be emphasized enough.

Today's world is beset with rapid changes in culture, government, technology, social mores, expectations, and economic concerns. "It is important that awake people be awake," poet William Stafford writes,[2] exhorting us to stay connected to our truest values and to each other.

The problem with answering a wake-up call is that we may not like the world we wake up to. The real crisis occurs when we interpret the world as so awful that it discourages us back to sleep—and we don't trust in ourselves or each other to have what it takes to work together to find solutions. We disagree on what "better" even looks like. When the issues are so layered and deep, it can be hard to know where to start.

That's why we need leaders with courage. Courage is first what it takes to open the door to reality and walk through. And more courage is required to stay on that side of reality, still in the game, wide awake.

Leading in a VUCA World

In a 2016 interim report titled *Thinking the Unthinkable: A New Imperative for Leadership in the Digital Age,* the authors Nik Gowing and Chris Langdon say, "There is clearly a sense of growing uncertainty, a sense of growing inability, a sense of lack of governance, a sense of lack of capability to grapple with these issues which show up without warning all of a sudden."[3] Besides the 2008 global financial crisis, the report names 2014 as "the great wake up" citing Putin seizing Crimea;

the so-called Islamic State seizing Mosul; the 60 percent drop in oil prices; the outbreak of Ebola; cyber attacks; and refugees and migrants fleeing Africa, Asia, and the Middle East, threatening the survival of the European Union.

The acronym VUCA describes this world: volatile, uncertain, complex, and ambiguous. Unthinkable events supposedly cannot be predicted or thought of in advance. You might say, "We don't know what we don't know." The leaders they interviewed observed, however, that most such events are better described as "unpalatable" elephant-in-the-room issues, ones that we ignore, discount, bypass, or do not report. One banker interviewed for the *Thinking the Unthinkable* report said, "Everyone went over the cliff edge at the same time" because "the contagion wasn't classically economical or financial, it was sociological." In other words, the authors note, "a banking crisis revealed something much deeper: denial and willful blindness, even if the looming reality was known." A CEO said, "What we're talking about—I don't know how you would engineer it—[is] a culture change towards just greater courage. Personal integrity and courage. Any business person will tell you, and does, that unless you are prepared to run the risk of failure, you're not likely to succeed."

Leadership Beyond Fight or Flight

How do we equip and sustain ourselves to adapt and thrive in a world that feels so volatile, uncertain, complex, and ambiguous? Much of how we respond depends on our biology and our conditioning.

When our stressed bodies perceive danger, our primitive amygdala goes into survival mode, overriding our newer prefrontal cortex known as the executive brain. A number of things happen: We narrow our focus into tunnel vision aimed at the threat, losing sight of the bigger picture. We focus on negatives and lose sight of positives and possibilities. We lose access to creativity in favor of well-established habits ingrained in our neural networks.

Complex cocktails of hormones geared toward survival wash through our body, limiting empathy and compassion, priming us for aggression, withdrawal, or paralysis. Other body processes shut down, leaving us unable to cry, digest, or eliminate, and sex drive is either lost or dysfunctional.[4] For each response, there's a behavioral spectrum ranging from positive to negative.

Fight. The fight response may show up as arguing one's own point, refusing to hear another opinion. Or as hostile aggression. Or it can look like mean-spirited competition turned toxic and sour, making siloes spring up to pose as safe havens. Inner anguish unchecked wreaks havoc and causes violence, pain, and suffering. Yet on the positive side, we fight for our rights, for our freedom, for the sake of survival, for the protection of others. Fighting positively in leadership can look like having somebody's back, standing up to a bullying boss, speaking truth to power.

Flight. Flee. Run away! When people storm out or hang up on a conversation or tense situation, they are fleeing a perceived danger, and it usually leaves bad feelings behind. If that response goes unaddressed and unresolved, it can cause even deeper mistrust and dissension. Sometimes there are good reasons to leave a situation without regret, including when you're simply ready to grow somewhere else. Some people come to a point where they must muster the courage to leave because of toxic or unhealthy circumstances. When a situation is futile and soul sucking, the best action is to protect yourself body and soul and move on.

Freeze. Often described as being like a deer caught in headlights, the freeze response to a threat is an instinctive prey response; we stop moving so as not to be seen by the predator. Freezing also shows up as unreadable stoic faces, an inability to think or speak clearly, indecision, unwillingness to have hard conversations, and not moving forward on projects that seem too complex to see what next step make sense. Yet freezing, reframed in the positive, might mean pausing instead. You can take a moment, an evening, or longer to gather your thoughts, become aware of emotions, and see the whole picture, including how other people are responding.

Flock. This stress reaction can be seen in the positive as tend-and-befriend and collaboration but in the negative as cliques, groupthink, and the exclusionary polarized mentality of us versus them. Peer pressure is another way to think of this. In his book *The Brain's Behind It,* Alistair Smith describes flocking as adopting the norms, values, and behavior of the peer group, or "herd." When children belong to a group that promotes indifference, for example, they will not display enthusiasm or curiosity, or admit they don't know an answer.[5] How often have you see that among adults in the workplace?

Fortitude and Courage

Fight. Flee. Freeze. Flock. But for each stress reaction, an option exists to get us out of our corners: *fortify.* As when we take vitamins and essential minerals, we can fortify ourselves for the hard times. When fortified, we can choose how to respond instead of simply reacting, and our choices come from a healthier, more self-aware stance.[6]

Fortitude is another word for courage. When Thomas Aquinas wrote about bravery in the thirteenth century, he used the Latin word *fortitudo,* and held that courage was a disposition required for every other virtue.[7] That was before the common usage of the French word *coeur* or the Latin *cor,* which translates as "heart."[8] Combine them both and think "strength of heart."

What are ways you fortify yourself on all levels, especially your heart? Mindfulness meditation, listening to good music, eating great food, dancing or running, spending time in nature, time spent with friends? Anything you do to regain your strength and composure, your clarity about who you are deep down inside, is a form of fortification. Self-awareness fortifies you to stand firm in your values. Doing meaningful work that reflects who you are gives you energy to work through hard times. Community fortifies you with kind support and the compassionate challenge of others. Strengthened, you find courage to act on the insights you've gained.

What inspires you, infuses you, instills you with the spirit of courage? Where in your body do you feel the urge to do the right thing no matter how hard? When do you know you must try without knowing whether or not you'll succeed? How do you tap into courage when you need it? Somehow you trust in your gut, you get up your nerve, you know in your heart, and your head clearly agrees.

To answer these questions and to see how to fortify yourself for the challenge ahead, it helps to understand that there's more than one kind of courage.

> "Be not afraid" does not mean we cannot *have* fear. Everyone has fear, and people who embrace the call to leadership often find fear abounding. Instead, the words say we do not need to *be* the fear we have.
>
> —Parker J. Palmer

Four Kinds of Courage

Different circumstances call for different ways of being courageous. We normally limit our thoughts about courage to physical or moral courage. But we can expand that understanding to the four categories of courage that appear in Rollo May's 1975 book, *The Courage to Create:* physical, moral, social, and creative courage.

Physical Courage

Perhaps the kind of courage we most often think of when we hear the word, physical courage enables us to use our bodies to go bravely into the fray, whether to fight for injustice, battle cancer, respond to an emergency, live with chronic illness or pain, or challenge our bodies to do more than normal. There's a sense of a willingness to risk injury or death for the sake of another or for the sake of our own survival or growth. It's a willingness to risk or endure an unpredictable measure of pain.

Physical courage is commonly applied to military heroism or "valor in the face of the enemy." Physical courage is not without some degree of thought or intention, however. Don't mistake physical courage for brashness or bravado, that form of derring-do that may have more to do with feeding your ego or being afraid to look less than you are.

Physical courage isn't always something you take time to think through. You just do it, as when Sigrid pulled herself up the steep hill after her car accident. And you're grateful later, looking back, that you did.

Some days it takes courage to wake up and get out of bed to go face the harsh realities that seem overwhelming even before you open your eyes. Then there is courage to make good choices and to live with the consequences of your choices that weren't so good. The courage to survive isn't something heroic, per se, but real life takes courage, nevertheless.

A former soldier tasked with rescuing hostages told me how the courage to risk your life for another is a *choice.*

It's a combination of physical and moral courage: "Clearly knowing the consequences and the likely harm to come to yourself, you proceed anyway, driven by an instinctive, inexplicable, undeniable sense of duty to the well-being of others, and even though a tremor of doom ripples through your body, you feel empowered at that moment simply because you have a choice in that moment, and those you may save don't."

Moral Courage

Moral courage is about the righting of wrongs, taking the risk to speak truth to power, to demand change and face the consequences. Movements for social change draw on this kind of courage when regular people decide to "live divided no more," as Parker Palmer puts it. Rosa Parks, Nelson Mandela, Harvey Milk, and, more recently, Malala Yousafzai all come to mind. At twelve, Malala began speaking up for girls' education in Pakistan, railing against the Taliban first in a school speech, then as an anonymous blogger for the

BBC, continuing after her identity was revealed. The Taliban issued a death threat against her, yet she continued to speak out. Yousafzai was fifteen and riding a bus home from school when a masked gunman boarded the bus demanding to know which girl was Malala. He shot her and her friends, but she survived. On her sixteenth birthday, she spoke to the United Nations General Assembly: "They thought that the bullets would silence us, but they failed. And out of that silence came thousands of voices. The terrorists thought they would change my aims and stop my ambitions. But nothing changed in my life except this: weakness, fear, and hopelessness died. Strength, power, and courage was born. I am the same Malala."[9]

People who express moral courage for the sake of highly visible change inspire everyday people to stand up for themselves and for others in countless everyday ways. Moral courage comes to ordinary people too, all the time, in less visible ways: Whistleblowers who risk not only their jobs but also their safety and more. Leaders who make business decisions based on moral values, not the fiscal bottom line. Employees who point out toxic organizational cultures and demand change. There are private moments of moral courage, when we know deep inside that the brave choice is correct because it's simply the right thing to do.

Fear of difference calls for a courageous response. One leader gave an example of moral and physical courage combined: "My sense of courage is framed by the extreme racism and institutional bias of growing up in America. It's an inner orientation, a way of finding courage and hope and wisdom from within, which was almost a given if you wanted to survive.

"When I'm in an elevator, I am mindful of who's in there with me, so I'm not unintentionally creating fear or dread because of my presence. Even walking down the street. It's part of my consciousness, especially at night. I won't walk behind people, particularly nonblack people, especially women, but even black women. Because I walk fast, I have to pay attention so I don't walk up behind someone as an African American male on a dark street."

Although that may sound like mindfulness or situational awareness, it's courage combined with a complex stance of hope and wisdom instead of hate and cynicism.

Social Courage

Social courage is one type of courage few people have explicitly named, although such researchers as Brené Brown are making the concept more common.[10] We exhibit social courage when we risk being vulnerable for the sake of relating to others with authentic presence. It means overcoming shame and risking loss, grief, embarrassment, sorrow, or disappointment for the possibility of love, joy, happiness, and connection. It takes courage to risk finding a place to belong. Without social courage, there is isolation, inauthentic connection, and lack of trustworthy relationships.

When we are willing to pay attention to our own emotions, to understand how we feel and express it (without using it as an excuse for poor behavior or choices), we become more authentic. And being authentic builds trust. Trust in oneself leads to being trustworthy with others. When we trust each other to do the right thing, we trust that by working together we can make a difference. We trust that our differences will contribute to better solutions. Social courage is about showing up as whole people and making it safe for others to show up, too. That's when we'll see real engagement and innovation in the workplace.

In a TEDx Talk called "Unmasking Masculinity," psychologist Ryan McKelley talks about the social conditioning of men that gives the message that emotions such as sorrow or grief are weak and inappropriate to reveal, whereas anger is seen as valid for men (but not women) to express. "There are places we find ourselves where emotional control and restriction is necessary," he says, showing an image of a firefighter with flames in the background. "But my concern is that the blocking and masking of emotions is our default mode in our human relationships, with workplace, families, and friendships."[11]

Creative Courage

Creative courage is the least recognized type of courage, but may be the one we need to cultivate most of all. It's the courage to come up with creative solutions, to create community, to create meaning from challenges, to create new visions and symbols that other people can rally around, and to create change that moves us forward in our humanity.

Sometimes creative courage means instigating change from within the institutions and organizations that need to be called back to their original intention to serve the greater good. Sometimes it means leaving a job you've outgrown, starting your own business, or becoming a change agent in other ways. It can also mean the courage to create a new life when the one you expected isn't the one you are facing.

Being creative means claiming your place at the table, saying you have what it takes and your voice needs to be heard. Being creative means painting your vision of what needs to be different, going for it, and inspiring others to take action, too. Being creative means leading the way with new ideas, new ways to act with integrity to achieve sustainable change.

That's why we need people who are artists at *heart,* while their *heads and hands* are willing to create change and solutions of all kinds around the globe. Connecting to your own form of artful, wholehearted leadership brings out your gifts for creating positive change.

Creative Courage Leads to Collective Courage

Sigrid's creative courage showed up in how she transformed the way her organization ran Santa Barbara's Earth Day event. "What I really needed was a production team that could carry out the logistics. It was like hosting a wedding party every year for thirty thousand people and everybody thinks they are the bride or the groom." Sigrid looked to community for an answer.

She invited a few small entrepreneurial production companies to a meeting and asked, "What do you guys want to do together? Let's go have some fun." The result was a revitalized Earth Day that has continued to thrive ever since, thanks to collaboration.

As time went on, Sigrid's creative courage expanded beyond her organization. "I became more interested in how we transform the sector as a whole."

Through the network of local nonprofit leaders that Sigrid had stayed involved with, she got acquainted with Erik Talkin, CEO of the Foodbank of Santa Barbara County. "Our paths might never have crossed. But in talking we recognized that the food system isn't working for people or the environment, that there was opportunity to do something together." Together they created a broad and diverse effort to examine the growing, harvesting, processing, packing, transporting, selling, and eating of food as well as the disposing of food waste.

"We asked, 'What could be done? What are you working on? Where's our potential role or niche?' We aimed to partner coming from this place of trust." With that trust and a lot of hard work over two years, the group launched the Food Action Plan in May 2016. It outlines actionable goals and strategies that will help build a more prosperous and resilient food system for people in Santa Barbara County.

If you're the courageous CEO, like Sigrid, then you're the one setting the tone. Does that always translate top-down into a creative, courageous workforce? Depending on the culture of a workplace, different types of courage will show up.

Cultivating Courage at Work

Monica Worline is an organizational psychologist who has studied courage and compassion in the workplace. She examined the ways in which people experience courage or failures of courage in terms of speaking up or staying silent. Her research wasn't about the big courage of whistleblowing, but the daily courage that allows people to risk being the person who stands up to say, "I know this project plan won't work" or "It feels like we're agreeing to something we don't all believe in."

Worline asked her subjects to tell a story of courage in their workplace. Eighty percent of the people told stories of seeing someone else act in a way they viewed as courageous. So she asked *those* people about their courage. They could see how someone might call their actions courageous, but would also explain how they saw it instead: "Oh, that was easy for me because I have a good relationship with my boss." Or they would refer to competence, saying, "I've done the same thing countless times in my previous job, so I knew it could be done."

Not recognizing or acknowledging our own courage isn't simply a matter of humility. When we examine our own behavior, we have access to our own interior landscape. We know that what looks risky from the outside isn't necessarily that risky inside.

"Just because you don't see this thing you did as extra courageous doesn't mean courage doesn't exist," Worline told me. "Courage exists in the space where people see others as exemplars. That is a generative tension. It doesn't erase the effect of that courage in the social space."

Courage exists in the spaces between us. That's worth repeating and imagining. Courage is not only in our hearts: when it happens and is witnessed, it becomes part of the space between us. Poet John O'Donohue speaks of blessing the space between us, of that moment when courage is kindled and we learn to find ease with risk.[12] A leader's job—and anyone who does this is leading—is to give encouragement to others, to help them recognize that they have more capacity than they realize.

If courage is not witnessed and interpreted as courage, does it count? The role of the witness does make a difference. Having your courage witnessed by others reinforces your resolve for the future, which is fortifying. Yet this thought from Mary Ann Radmacher is true, too: "Courage does not always roar. Sometimes courage is the quiet voice at the end of the day saying, 'I will try again tomorrow.'"[13]

How Organizations Influence Courage

In her years of studying organizational psychology, Worline sees that courage shows up differently depending on the context of the organization itself. Something about the structure and culture of organizations changes the stories people tell about courage in the workplace.[14]

In top-down organizations, courage looks like pushing back against the hierarchy or standing up to people in authority with a different opinion. Stories of failure or lack of courage often come from organizations where people don't think the organization stands for much, or cares only about making money.

But in organizations that foster strong autonomy and lots of opportunity without micromanagement, a more constructive courage emerges. In those conditions where the organization's purpose is clear and shared, courage tends to look like people discovering something they want to make happen, something they believe in, and taking the initiative to make it happen. Courage looks like becoming a project champion or "raising the bar."

The social courage to connect heart-to-heart shows up as compassion in the workplace. It entails vulnerability and also relational trust. In her book *Awakening Compassion at Work,* Worline calls this courage a form of "fierce compassion" that involves refusing to perpetuate suffering in work situations. It takes courage to let people go or to speak honestly about unacceptable behavior.[15] Courage is required for standing up to disrespect and incivility and intervening to stop people from manipulating the system.[16] Although this sounds like moral courage, it is someone taking action on behalf of the social group and because of a deep caring about what's at stake for the organization or what is central to the mission and values.

One isn't necessarily born with courage, but one is born with potential. Without courage, we

cannot practice any other virtue with consistency. We can't be kind, true, merciful, generous, or honest.
—Maya Angelou

Courage Comes from True Self

If courage is needed for being a leader, how can you become more of a person who does lead the way? (It's both *can* and *do.*) What is inside the person who leads, not just with physical bravery but with moral, social, and creative courage?

Courage is what happens when you bring inspiration and integrity to your decisions to take action. Courage is the life force that animates you in moments of decision and action. Courage is what happens when your soul shows up. Courage is not only *in* you—it is you. In your moments of courage, you meet your true self.

What Is the Courage Way?

> Our complicity in world making is a source of awesome and sometimes painful responsibility—and a source of profound hope for change. It is the ground of our common call to leadership, the truth that makes leaders of us all.
> —Parker J. Palmer

Most people would agree that leadership is something we need more of, but there's little agreement about exactly what good leadership means, except that we don't want more of the traditionally hierarchical and authoritarian style. Search the Internet with the keywords *good leadership* and you'll find countless books and articles with lists of the top skills and traits of a good leader. You'll also find all kinds of programs and coaches and organizations claiming to offer *the* secrets to leading well, as if there were a shortcut.

Most of us know "good" leadership when we see it or experience it; we put labels on it, like *authentic, transformational, trustworthy, successful, courageous.* Look further. Good leadership is about making good decisions by balancing inevitable tensions and knowing when to take risks. Leadership is keeping your values in sight regardless of the pressures around you, and staying calm in the storms that arise. Leadership is listening well and inviting opinions and answers from others. Leadership is inspiring others with your vision, influencing them with the power of your presence. Leadership encourages others to step into their leadership, too.

That's a lot to expect from a leader, yet that's what is required, both for the running of organizations and institutions and for those who aspire to create change in the world despite broad disagreement on precisely what needs to change. Good leaders shape the conversation so that meaningful progress can be made around complex issues.

Leadership can be exhausting, lonely, frustrating, disappointing, ineffective, and downright discouraging. To sustain themselves, leaders need stamina, inner strength, and a supportive community.

So where do you find such resources for good leadership? Lists of traits and skills may tell you what kind of leader to be, but they don't tell you how to get there. At its core, leadership is a daily, ongoing practice, a journey toward becoming your best self and inviting others to do the same. And at the heart of this daily practice is courage. And that's where the Courage Way comes in. It's a guide to leadership and a way of life that names and explores this important resource and shows leaders how to access and draw on courage in all that they do.

The Heart of Leadership

We might sense that courage comes from within, but really, how do we find it or draw on it? To answer this, Parker Palmer and the Center for Courage &

Renewal explore the essential questions: *What if courage comes from a deep trust in ourselves, a trust rooted in profound self-knowledge?* And not just from ego- or mind-based thinking but from the deepest part of ourselves, where we can be true to ourselves and true to others. *What if more people made choices based on a mindful, self-aware way of weighing the options, seeing the biggest picture, and consciously considering the feelings and opinions of others, while staying faithful to a much larger vision of purpose and meaning?*

In fact, the realization of these "what ifs" can be seen in the history of social movements when the power of the human heart is skillfully evoked and deployed in strategic action that counters the power of positional authority and physical prowess and economic might. If that were not the case, no oppressed minorities would ever have made any social gains. These are movements animated by the only power left to people who have had all the external power taken away from them: the heart to claim their integrity.

If the heart weren't so powerful, there would never have been social movements to rectify social injustices. If the heart weren't so powerful in its commitment to meaning and purpose and caring for others, the ongoing need to collaborate, to reach common understandings, and to work out the details, movements would be unable to effect meaningful change.

For over twenty-five years, the Center for Courage & Renewal, its facilitators, its staff, and the thousands of people who have gone through its programs have been exploring these "what-if" questions and have come up not with answers but with a way of living, thinking, relating, and leading that is life giving. The Courage Way is at the center of what it takes to empower people to lead in wholehearted ways, regardless of the scale and scope of their efforts.

Five Key Ingredients of the Courage Way

In the more than 120 interviews I conducted for this book, I found a pattern of five key ingredients in how leaders have learned to cultivate courage. Three powerful main concepts are true self, trust, and community; the two key practices are paradox and reflection. Later chapters will flesh out each idea, but here's a brief overview.

True Self

Our basic premise is that inside of each person is the essential self who continues to grow and yet somehow, deep down, remains constant. Every person has access to this inner source of truth, named in various wisdom traditions as identity and integrity, inner teacher, heart, inner compass, spirit, or soul. Your true self is a source of guidance and strength that helps you find your way through life's complexities and challenges. When you begin to listen to and trust the truest part of yourself, your choices and relationships flow from that trust, begetting more trust.

Trust

Courage takes trust—in ourselves and in each other. Trustworthy relationships create the conditions for people to flourish and for positive change to arise. Relational trust is based on our perceptions of personal regard, professional respect, competence, and integrity in other people. Coming to understand the attitudes, assumptions, and biases that lead to such perceptions of trust entails honest inner work. Our collection of principles and practices is a time-tested approach for facilitating inner work and cultivating relational trust.

Community

Becoming more self-aware and trustworthy requires both individual introspection and a supportive community. We offer a specialized meaning of community as "solitudes alone together" as well as a "community of inquiry." Our practices offer models for how to reflect and interact with each other so that new clarity and courage can emerge.

Being receptive to the very idea of needing other people in community takes courage and yet, in turn, creates resilience. Leaders must know how to invite people into and hold them accountable for cocreating trustworthy space so that they can support each other in service of their work together. Achieving effective collaboration requires genuine trustworthy community.

Paradox

We can learn to practice paradox by recognizing that the polarities that come with being human (life and death, love and loss) are "both-ands" rather than "either-ors." We can learn to let those tensions hold us in ways that stretch our hearts and minds open to new insights and possibilities. With paradox we honor both the voice of the individual *and* our collective intelligence. We trust both our intellects *and* the knowledge that comes through our bodies, intuitions, and emotions. Paradox values both speaking *and* listening. An appreciation of paradox enriches our lives, helping us hold greater complexity. Integrating our inner lives with our work in the world comes from daily practice in holding paradox.

Reflection

Reflection cultivates more ways of knowing and learning that complement your mind and emotions, but draw from a deeper place: your intuition, imagination, and innermost being. Reflection is a practice that can be enriched by the mirroring of trustworthy companions.

When we reflect together, such as by exploring how universal stories of human experience intersect with the personal stories of our lives, it can create relational trust. Guided conversations focused on a poem, a teaching story, a piece of music, or a work of art—drawn from diverse cultures and wisdom traditions—invite us to reflect on the big questions of our lives, allowing each person to explore them in his or her own way. Reflection helps us find the inner ground on which we stand firm, and it helps us find common ground with others.

If we are willing to embrace the challenge of becoming whole, we cannot embrace it all alone—at least, not for long: we need trustworthy relationships to sustain us, tenacious communities of support, if we are to sustain the journey toward an undivided life. Taking an inner journey toward rejoining soul and role requires a rare but real form of community that I call a "circle of trust."
—Parker J. Palmer

Creating a Container for Trust

We spend so many hours of our day and week in the workplace, we need and want it to feed our well-being on many levels: mental, physical, emotional, and spiritual. Trust is a key to well-being. If the idea of creating trustworthy space for yourself and for your colleagues sounds appealing, you may be wondering how you can do that consistently—or how you can sustain it.

The hallmark of the Center for Courage & Renewal's work is its emphasis on the Circle of Trust® approach,[1] the purpose of which is to create and sustain safe space for individuals and the group they are part of. Circle practices have existed for as long as humans have had fires to gather around and language to talk with one another. Contemporary circle practices have developed for personal growth, restorative justice, team building, peacemaking, community building, and so on. Circles of Trust were developed to help participants "reconnect soul and role," to renew their passion for their profession, and as time went on it became clear that our approach also created relational trust among people. Our circles are facilitated using a set of rules called touchstones.

Touchstones are our operating guidelines for holding the meaningful conversations of inner work and trust building. They form strong boundaries for interactions and are designed to disrupt the typical hierarchy and power dynamics often seen in workplace conversations. These touchstones can also be adapted to define how you work together with integrity and trust in an organization, community, or network—inviting the best of each person to show up and contribute.

You'll see touchstones mentioned throughout the book, as leaders describe how the practices came into play in their situation and/or organization. Take a moment to soak in these ideas; find someone to compare notes with about these different ways of relating to yourself and to others.

Each touchstone alone is an admirable idea. You could devote a day to noticing how it shows up in your life or work; you could meditate on each one for a week or a month. The magic and mystery of this collection of practices comes from the chemistry of how they combine to catalyze trust.

Together, these touchstones create a hospitable "container," one that enables people to show up with integrity and authenticity so that they can engage in honest conversation. I use the word *container* consciously. How do we create containers that hold people—relationships, corporate culture, community—accountable? How do we hold people with regard and respect? For that, good ground rules are needed, and that's what the touchstones are. Here I've included a short version of them to start; we'll explore them in a little more detail in the rest of the chapter.

TOUCHSTONES AT A GLANCE

1. Give and receive welcome.
2. Be present as fully as possible.
3. Extend invitation, not demand.
4. Speak your truth in ways that respect other people's truth.
5. No fixing, saving, advising, or correcting each other.
6. When the going gets rough, turn to wonder.
7. Practice asking open, honest questions.
8. Attend to your own inner teacher.
9. Trust and learn from the silence.

10. Commit to and maintain confidentiality.

11. Know that it's possible for the seeds planted here to keep growing.

At the deepest levels of human life, we do not need techniques. We need insights into ourselves and our world that can help us understand how to learn and grow from our experiences of diversity, tension, and conflict.

—Parker J. Palmer

Touchstones for Creating Trustworthy Space

Touchstones can be grouped into three phases for building trust and thus courage, both within yourself and with others—intention, interaction, and integration.

Intention

The first three touchstones suggest ways to practice *welcome, presence,* and *invitation* as you enter into any interaction. Each one calls on your self-awareness and intention. Together they set the tone for relational trust to emerge, like playing middle C to tune a piano or inviting choir voices to come together around a single pitch. These touchstones can define the tonality of your personal leadership and your organizational culture.

Give and Receive Welcome

Extend hospitality, and presume welcome, too. This includes welcome and support for diverse perspectives, opinions, and approaches. Welcome moves us from loneliness toward belonging. When we feel welcome, we are more likely to learn, engage, and contribute to collective efforts.

Be Present as Fully as Possible

Set aside the usual distractions of voicemail, e-mail, things undone from yesterday, things to do tomorrow. Bring all of yourself—your doubts, fears, and failings as well as your convictions, joys, and successes, your listening as well as your speaking—to the work, not just the parts of yourself and your experience that would be obviously relevant to this work.

Practices which demonstrate that you are fully paying attention are a rare gift in these days of multitasking and competing priorities. But being present means more than that. This touchstone gives you a chance to honor the wholeness of life, to acknowledge the complexities inside you and all that you're facing. It's a way of saying, "Despite all that is happening in my life right now, I am committed to being focused on our work at this moment to the best of my ability." And because we're all human, we can relate.

Extend Invitation, Not Demand

In a Circle of Trust, participation in conversation is always by invitation, never by demand. Participation by listening with care is no less a contribution than participation by speaking with care.

Inner work must be invitational because the inner teacher speaks by choice, not on command. We all need times and places where there is the freedom within a purposeful process to learn and grow in our own way, on our own schedule, and at our own level of need.

Some people appreciate the phrase "This is not a share-or-die event," especially those who are more introverted or just plain tired. Interestingly enough, when participation is invitational, people are even more likely to eventually join in. In the workplace, this authentic invitation to participate means a commitment to actively engage one another in the common work and avoid making anyone feel coerced, whether in a conversation or a process.

It seems counterintuitive to consider invitation as a valid practice in the workplace, where people are paid and expected to do their work. Subordinates may resist being asked to step up, preferring directives instead. Followers, by contrast, want to be motivated by a personal and meaningful challenge. They will rise to the occasion of authentic and consistent invitation from a strong and compassionate leader. How might you invite but not insist that others step into their own leadership and potential?

Interaction

The next touchstones are meant to guide interactions during dialogue and large-group conversations. But they are just as applicable to your daily life and how you treat other people at work and at home.

Speak Your Truth in Ways That Respect Other People's Truth

This touchstone asks you to use "I" statements and to respect that views of reality may differ. It is applicable in friendships, personal and mentoring relationships, and other situations where sharing your genuine story is what matters most. When you're getting to know people, it's vital to share stories across lines of difference, not to debate who's right or wrong, and not to cast blame or shame.

Imagine a workplace where you are invited to speak your truth and to share your knowledge, gifts, and expertise, trusting that your voice will be heard and your contribution respected.

Deliberations about direction, priorities, approaches, money, leadership, and power do elicit many facets of truth from members of the group. It is therefore important that people be able to speak their perspective and truth and be responsible in communicating it to others.

In the workplace, especially when solving problems, it's healthy and necessary to interpret and debate what others say. Speaking with "I" statements can improve discussion and decision-making, encourage respectful listening, and safeguard against aspects of social exchange that make a person feel unsafe.

No Fixing, Saving, Advising, or Correcting Each Other

This touchstone goes back to the premise that our true self knows best. Leaders (and elders, bosses, spouses, siblings, and friends) often feel expected to have all the answers. This is one of the hardest guidelines to follow no matter what the role or job title because we are conditioned to believe that we are being helpful when we offer each other advice.

But aren't leaders *supposed* to fix, save, advise, and correct their team, peers, and even their bosses? This touchstone doesn't mean avoiding giving advice when it is definitely needed. Good leaders point their team in a direction where they can find answers, and also instill the belief that team members have the gifts and capacity to make good decisions the leaders will support.

This touchstone reframes our response from counsel to curiosity, from invasiveness to inquiry, especially when combined with the other touchstones. As countercultural as this touchstone is, it is also the one that leaders cited as among the most valuable, along with the next one, turning to wonder.

When the Going Gets Rough, Turn to Wonder

If you feel judgmental or defensive in the midst of an interaction, pause long enough to ask yourself, *I wonder what brought her to this belief? I wonder what he's feeling right now? I wonder what my reaction teaches me about myself?* This practice allows you to set aside judgment to listen to others—and to yourself—with compassionate inquiry.

Some leaders say they prefer to ponder their own reaction first, which is vital to cultivating deeper self-awareness and owning their reactions. In the heat of the moment during a discussion, however, it might serve the conversation to simply turn to wonder about the other person's reaction so that you intentionally set aside judgment and stay present enough to listen.

Many participants tell us that turning to wonder is one of the touchstones they use most in their life. It's a way of offering grace to another, of allowing for moments when they're not at their best. By wondering what's going on inside someone else, you can be generous with another. You can give leeway when a casual remark stings like an insult, even if delivered without harmful intention or not even directed at you. And it encourages a sense of reciprocity when you can expect this same treatment from your colleagues on your own hard days.

In the workplace, it is important to have ways to voice disagreement, respectfully talk about the differences, and move toward resolution. Trust among members is never more important than during times of confusion or disagreement. Sometimes leaders must hold that wonder until there is an appropriate time, and safe space, to follow up on an issue. There's a time and a place to confront other people, though *confront* is not the right word. You can choose to approach others as a diplomat. This leads to the next touchstone: asking open, honest questions.

Practice Asking Open, Honest Questions

Instead of offering advice or holding on to wonder so long that it becomes unproductive, you can seek understanding. Open, honest questions are ones you cannot possibly know the answer to in advance; they are meant to elicit insights, to help people access their own resourcefulness.

Practical uses of open, honest questions range from a different way to structure performance evaluations to deep discernment about life transitions. There is an art to asking questions that are not leading or directive, and we'll go into this practice in detail in chapter 8.

Attend to Your Own Inner Teacher

As you listen to and interact with others, pay close attention to your own reactions and responses. Growing more socially and emotionally self-aware is the essence of building trust in yourself. Attending to your inner teacher is a form of mindfulness that includes listening in to your body and gut (through which your true self sends signals), and also checking in with your wisest companion at your core. When such reflective practice becomes second nature—and is used to monitor your reactions throughout a stressful day—you become more resilient, responsive, and real.

Trust and Learn from the Silence

Silence, or stillness, is a gift in our noisy world and a way of knowing in itself. It is all too rare in organizational settings where team or group members may compete for airtime and visibility, so this practice may seem hard to incorporate into such settings. Yet silence is vital to allowing each person's inner wisdom to emerge and all voices to be heard and valued. Silence in this context is not the same thing as being silenced, an experience of oppressed and marginalized people or in situations where power dynamics come into play.

It takes practice to be comfortable with more than a few seconds of generative silence before people begin to fidget or speak up. Silence has its own momentum that can lead to breakthrough insights if held long enough. Interrupting silence too soon may shut down valuable comments that will otherwise never emerge.

Silence and spaciousness can add value to workplace processes. Silence informs the best steps to take next, brings focus back to the group, and increases people's patience with the process and with different paces of learning and responding. After someone has spoken, take time to reflect without immediately filling the space with words. Having a spacious agenda and providing space through breaks or by moving to another topic when needed allow participants to "sit with" questions or issues until there is a new understanding. Also helpful is to have methods in place to hold the questions and return to them at regular intervals, something as simple as a "parking lot" list on a flipchart or whiteboard.

Integration

The final two touchstones are the takeaways, the commitments to protecting trustworthy space and integrating your insights long after the day's conversation has come to a close.

Commit to and Maintain Confidentiality

People are more likely to trust each other and their leaders when they know that their words and stories will remain with those with whom they choose to share them, and will never be passed on to others without permission.

People who practice confidentiality can be trusted. Leaders and colleagues who gossip cannot. Of course, there are situations (and professions) where people have a legal obligation to report that someone is being harmed or is in danger. When something has been shared in confidence, we must be able to discern when to bring an issue to light, or encourage others to speak up for themselves.

More than one leader we interviewed mentioned the value of experiencing fierce attention to confidentiality, not just for others but for themselves. Many leaders feel isolated and unable to speak frankly about doubts and emotions, except in therapeutic situations or perhaps with a trusted spouse or close friend. The touchstone of confidentiality, when honored among colleagues or in leadership cohorts, gives leaders a way to build trust and experience trust. This can then translate into knowing whom they can trust when it's time to collaborate.

Know That It's Possible for the Seeds Planted Here to Keep Growing

Ponder this one as a metaphor. This touchstone can mean trusting in the seasons of your career: there is often a time lag in deriving meaning from the most complex, challenging events, especially if you didn't seem to achieve success at the time. At the scale of long-term change, this touchstone is a reminder that your work unfolds over time and that you may not always see immediate results of your efforts. You might also apply it to the idea of vocation, when you know you've answered your calling to your fullest extent and you realize it's time to move on.

You can also apply this touchstone to moments of renewal, snatched snippets of sunlight when you can breathe in and out, perhaps listen to music, walk your dog, read a poem. Your busy life as a leader may mean that those moments are brief or too few, but if you drop into them with your full presence, you can trust that the seed of renewal you've planted will sustain you as you go on with your day.

One leader said she interprets this touchstone as "believing that when we move from this particular strategic planning process, we can leave this particular time and place more revived and renewed than when we first came into this conversation."

Another leader told me that it's simply the first four words of this touchstone that he finds the most aspirational: *know that it's possible.* He said, "Even in a world where national dialogue is increasingly uncivil and common ground seems more rare, I know that we are not emotionally or morally far from our shared values. I know that what is possible first presents itself in the heart, and then makes its way to the head. I know and perhaps fear that with each passing day, what is possible—at least from an ecological standpoint—might become less and less probable. And, of course, I know we stand in many tragic gaps in life, and recognize that our vocation lies somewhere between what is real and what can be."

No longer seen as having sole responsibility for finding a solution, leaders must engage others in understanding problems. It means facilitating—or holding space

for—the distress that comes with asking tough questions, appreciating the scope of the problem, reconsidering their current roles, and challenging comfortable norms.
—Deborah Helsing, Annie Howell, Robert Kegan, and Lisa Lahey

Holding Space

A leader's job is to hold space for the vision and purpose, to hold space for others to do their good work. Effective leaders hold space for conversation, especially on difficult issues with many points of view, and invite others to show up with their full abilities, ideas, and energy. It takes tenacity to hold the space in which people can discover their inner resources.

As we learned from Monica Worline's research cited in the introduction, courage exists in the spaces between us. When we craft spaces with intentionality in order to evoke creativity in the people who come into those spaces, it's a double helping of creativity. That's because people find courage to bring forth something new from within themselves *and* from between each other. As the poet Wendell Barry reminds us, "What we need is here."[2]

What's *within us* as individuals is foundational and critical. But when clarity and wisdom arise from the conversations *between us,* something happens: a shared and larger truth arises from the center of the circle. And from there, courage is born from the trust that's created. We find integrity and the courage to act on it.

Imagine the eleven touchstones arranged in a circle so that you can sense the container they create for meaningful conversation—and creativity—that can arise from within. Together the touchstones help leaders hold space, but not as dogma or rigid rules. More than the precise words used to describe them, it's the intention beneath each touchstone that matters.

Finding Your Own Way

These touchstones can do more than serve as guidelines for group process. They can go with you into your day, accessible and effective for helping you respond as a leader with more presence in moments of pressure, challenge, and tension.

For your personal leadership, you might think of these ideas as a cairn of stones you can stack on your desk to remind you of how you want to behave during the day-to-day grind. Just like a cairn, the touchstones fit together in a fine balance, but you must find your own way to arrange them.

Rest assured, the leaders you'll meet in this book don't always remember or refer to the touchstones by name but they've come to embody the concepts. It's one thing to know in your head what to do as a leader, another to cultivate these qualities inside your heart. There is no quick fix. That embodiment takes time and intention. The Courage Way is a lifelong practice in cultivating authenticity, meaning, and wholeness—and that takes practice *and* community. Our hope is that these pages inspire you to let your courage lead the way.

2

The Inner Work of Leadership

> The salvation of this human world lies nowhere else than in the human heart, in the human power to reflect, in human modesty, and in human responsibility.
> —Václav Havel

Ever since he was a little kid, Patrick Herson thought he would become a doctor. His father often told stories of the small-town general practitioners who delivered Patrick and his sisters. "I do have a sense of calling," Patrick told me, "but it was more about hero worship of the docs who took care of us. Becoming a doctor felt like something natural to do." He happily practiced medicine for years, delivering more than five hundred babies himself. He also took on added leadership roles. As time went on, he became frustrated trying to do both—and do both well.

Eventually Patrick realized he could have a greater impact on patients' health by leading the good work of others rather than by caring for patients directly. He became a medical director overseeing six hundred providers in Minnesota, where he found himself guiding and, as he says, "occasionally dragging" his medical group through a tumultuous period of change.

"Earlier in my career there were times when I had to do things to and with my patients that I knew would be difficult," Patrick said, naming examples such as giving immunizations or a spinal tap, or an aggressive childbirth because the baby was in trouble and needed to be born before a C-section could be done. "I could confidently know that it was done in the name of serving a patient and leading to a predictably better outcome."

But when he stepped into the director role, Patrick remembers thinking, *I'm not so confident I can point with assurance that everything will be better when all is said and done. How do I guide my group and myself through this?*

To get through those changes, Patrick knew he needed to continue to grow in mind, heart, and skill. And he needed likeminded and like-hearted leaders to turn to for encouragement. Patrick signed up for one of our six-month leadership programs (the Courage & Renewal Academy for Leaders) to give himself those resources. To his surprise, he found himself needing support more than ever when he was promoted quite suddenly to interim president of his medical group, responsible for leading two thousand employees.

"In my first two weeks I was feeling a little bolloxed by the responsibility. I remember having an image of this metaphor that I was standing on the top of a ten-meter diving platform ready to jump in. The pool itself represented bringing my whole self into my leadership role, living my life inside out, and bringing the passions that boil inside of me to that. I remember being aware I could just as easily back off down that platform, come down the stairs, and quietly slip into the pool. In many ways, that choice felt safer. I couldn't embarrass myself. I might land cattywampus. Yet it felt really important to take a running leap into the pool."

So he leapt into his new role, but did so with humility. "I often say to people, since I don't practice medicine anymore, that I'm the least useful employee we have in our medical group. Our patients are seen by about six hundred physicians and nurse practitioners, physician assistants, midwives, plus medical assistants, nurses, lab techs, X-ray techs, and so on. My role as a leader is creating a vision of what that patient care can look like and what is possible."

Patrick likens his role to that of an attentive gardener: "What should that garden look like? What do our patients need? What can we be providing for people? I can't make the vegetables grow; I just can do my best to be attentive to them and get the preparation right. The right seed, water when necessary, but then stand back and watch that kind of magic happen."

Patrick told me that he has attempted to create those right conditions by applying a variety of practices and mindsets, first for his own renewal: "For starters, I've just slowed down a little bit, which I think has been an important part of my leadership, to let people catch up with me, but also give myself a chance to catch up with my thoughts and ideas as well. I have more patience to step back a bit and be more observant of what's happening."

He has also brought specific practices into leading together with colleagues, and he sees the results ripple out. Many employees—medical directors, clinic administrators, physicians, and midwives—have attended Courage-based programs, so the practices are gaining traction throughout the organization.

"We use the touchstones from time to time. Not every month, but if I know that we're getting into a thorny topic or something that's really critical to our work, I'll stop and bring those out. It's a way to remind people that we're entering into a different kind of a dialogue, or there's a different intentionality to the conversation that I want to have. That's a nice way to just stop for a moment, review the touchstones, and then proceed with that work."

He intentionally tries to structure conversations so that people can feel a degree of safety. Curiosity paired with asking open, honest questions encourages people to express sincere doubts, concerns, or worries about the work.

"I often encourage people to be wonder-filled. Since doing so, I see more of that kind of inquiry instead of judgment. It's allowed us to have some better dialogue." More interactions center on questions like *Why do you see this problem this way? Why is the solution you're proposing a good one?*

"We recently had a really challenging strategic issue that we were facing about merging with part of the university. One day our CEO was feeling very beat up about the conversations, and I sent him a copy of Mary Oliver's poem 'The Journey.' He wrote me later and said, 'That was really nice to reframe what's happening.'"

That's an example of how a micro-shift of compassionate leadership can encourage others. "It's just trying to give a little nudge and redirect when possible, without having to do a lot of pulling and tugging myself." Because of his subtle modeling, some days Patrick has also received much-needed encouragement.

On another day, Patrick brought in a poem, Rainer Maria Rilke's "Go to the Limits of Your Longing," which has a line that says, "no feeling is final." That wasn't the line that struck Patrick the most when he first read it, but it flowed back to him with good will later that morning when the group got into a rough patch of conversation.

"We were hacking through something important for us, but it was tough going. I was getting a little frustrated and feeling a little off balance, and one of my physician leads said, 'Don't forget that line in the poem, Patrick. Not every feeling is final. This is going to get better.' I was so tickled that she had latched onto that and could offer it back to me as a little bit of a life buoy at that moment."

Is this person the same on the inside as he or she seems to be on the outside? Children ask this about their parents, students about their teachers, employees about their supervisors, patients about their physicians, and citizens about their political leaders. When the answer is yes, we relax, believing that we are in the presence of integrity and feeling secure enough to invest ourselves in the relationship and all that surrounds it.

—Parker J. Palmer

Leading from the Inside Out

The inner work of leadership depends on the strongest muscle in the human body: the heart. We mean heart in its ancient sense, "the place where intellect and emotion and spirit and will converge in the human self."[1] One way to visualize that convergence zone of courage is the Möbius strip.[2] Many leaders told me—their hands unconsciously drawing a horizontal figure eight as they spoke—of how this graphic model helps them stay aware of how their inner life influences their work. They talk of trying to be vigilant in maintaining the flow from inner to outer and outer to inner.

The Möbius strip is paradox personified. It represents the possibility of movement from a divided life to wholeness. Try this yourself:

Take a piece of paper and by cutting, folding, or tearing, make a long strip. Find a pencil or pen.

Let one side of the strip represent your outer or onstage life. Think of your image, persona, roles and responsibilities, influence, and impact. On this side of the strip, write down words or phrases that represent these aspects of your outer professional life and how others see you. You can include pressures, challenges, and problems that seem to land on your doorstep from the outside. What gives you privilege and power, or doesn't?

Let the other side of the strip represent your inner or backstage life. Think of your values, beliefs, ideas, hopes, and fears. Write down words about your inner, personal life—the parts of yourself that aren't as visible to others. What do you love? What would you fight for?

Now hold out this strip in your hands. You can see only one side at a time. Turn it over. Again. Regard what you've put on each side. Reflect for a moment on what you wrote down and why. The two sides seem completely separate—how could they be otherwise? The paradox is that they aren't always so separate. When we are born, we are undivided and whole. One can see this in newborns and little kids, with that wise light in their eyes, their cries of discomfort, their laughter full of delight. What you see is what you get! As we move into adolescence (and for some even sooner), the inner life becomes a place of fragile feeling and tender truth. As it dawns on us that the outer world is dangerous, we wall off and hide away that which is most precious. The side of us that is most private and personal is turned away from outer scrutiny, and we think we're safe. We try to hide our very private feelings of fear, passion, self-doubt, and uncertainty, hoping they don't spill out and embarrass us.

As we grow older, it's as if we are joining the two ends of our strip of paper so that it forms a circle that keeps the inner inside and the outer outside. There's a spectrum of experience on each dimension, but they are alone, enclosed, separated.

One word for this stage is "centering." A centered life is a step beyond the earlier dualism; we honor what's true for ourselves. But we've "circled the wagons" to confine inner truth to that which is familiar and comfortable, and exclude that which seems alien or challenging. This can prevent openhearted engagement with the rest of the world unless we invite it in, too.

But there's another way. Flatten the paper for a moment and give it one twist, then bring the ends back together, twist still intact. This creates a Möbius strip. If you run your finger around as though on a track and see where it goes, you'll find that it's on a continuous trek of three-dimensional space. This shape has only one side and only one edge! If you can get to a point where you are living your life as though you were on a Möbius strip, you can reclaim your birthright of wholeness.

If you are living on the Möbius strip, who you *are* is connected with what you *do.* Imagine yourself living and leading on this Möbius strip. Some days you might relax, "holed up" inside. Some days you run round as if on a racetrack. Sometimes you're stuck. Sometimes it seems you hang on that edge by a thread or your fingertips. But if you think of that single Möbius edge as your leadership growth edge, you may realize that despite everything hard going on, you can grow.

When we consciously connect the ends of that metaphorical paper and form a Möbius strip, we invite congruence and flow. Think of trust as the glue. We acknowledge that our inner lives do affect how we show up in the world. What happens outside, good or bad, flows back in, where it needs to be processed and integrated. It's the ongoing integration that matters, not being both places at once. Letting one aspect inform the other is a practice that is life changing—and life giving, especially for leaders.

At the Heart of the Work

The idea of courage as coming from the heart has inspired Patrick to talk with his team about holding patients "at the heart of their work" clinically.

"That's a nice place to be as a leader because it's hard for people to argue with you about that. It just naturally resonates with people who are drawn to health care. Being able to keep the frame and the focus on that, instead of the numbers, has been really, really helpful."

In describing the heart of his leadership, Patrick referred to the Möbius strip concept: "I really took to heart Parker's invitation to live your life inside out. To not hide that passion and what's inside of your life but to bring that into reality. It's there, showing up in other ways. Why not just be explicit about it?"

Patrick is one of many leaders who described being willing to wear their heart on their sleeve. Physicians especially spoke of their willingness to be vulnerable with their colleagues about their personal passion for patient care, whether that's by becoming an advocate for depressed patients, improving screening rates for breast cancer due to personal experience with loved ones, or managing hypertension or diabetes because of deaths in the family. Tapping into the reality of illnesses in any physician's family life, bringing that forward into dialogue, helps mitigate compassion fatigue, where protective emotional boundaries arise between physicians and their work.

"By allowing the reality of heartbreak and hope into strategy sessions, it becomes possible to avoid making decisions based on some cold, sterile, clinical prevalence or incidence. We can say, 'We've got to get our numbers up, because it's people like my daughter who are going to get better care and be leading lives that are healthier and better. We're going to detect cancers earlier for our mothers and our sisters and our daughters and our grandmothers, and they're going to have longer lives as a result of that.'"

The world needs competent people with the heart to keep showing up, day in and day out, and often on the night shift, to do the hard work. This inner work of embracing both passion and vulnerability is essential to cultivating a heart that can withstand all the pain and complexity and still show up to help make a difference.

Leaders like Patrick are adept at cultivating integrity for themselves and the people they work with and serve. Such integrity results from aligning insights both from the private conversations inside leaders' heads and hearts *and* the trust-building conversations leaders hold with other people.

We were created in and for a complex ecology of relatedness, and without it we wither and die. This simple fact has critical implications: community is not a goal to be achieved but a gift to be received.
—Parker J. Palmer

Receptiveness to Community

Leadership can be lonely, but it doesn't have to be. It requires not only a capacity to create community but also a willingness to *receive* community as a gift. Becoming receptive to the idea of needing a community is an act of social courage because it means allowing yourself to be real. Many leaders do not want to admit that they need help or have feelings or need other people. Such humility can be seen as weakness. Becoming receptive involves inner work. It must be present in you as "a capacity for connectedness"—a capacity to resist the forces of disconnection, such as narcissism, egotism, jealousy, and competition.

In the complicated landscape of your life, you may have community in one arena but not in another. At certain times in your life, you may be happily surrounded by colleagues, family, and friends; as circumstances change, you may find yourself alone once again. Community is rarely a given, obtained once and kept forever. As Patrick pointed out, community requires careful, regular tending, just as a garden does if it is to thrive for more than one season.

"I was keenly aware we didn't have as much fun together as I thought we probably should. I decided to recruit what we call the Fun Committee. There's three of us, and we have very fun planning meetings after hours in a local bar. Then we plan events, about one a quarter, for the senior executive team to do or to host for other executive groups. That sense of creating community has been really important, and helped us with some challenging work that we had to do in the first half of this year."

Cultivating community can also be a form of self-care. Patrick applies an adaptive leadership concept: giving yourself a sense of sanctuary on a daily, weekly, monthly, and annual basis.

"It's easy to feel you can't add anything new to your day, but this idea didn't require me to do something new, but just do what I'm doing with more intentionality." When stepping into the shower each morning or being more attentive at church, he says to himself, "This is my sanctuary."

"I play racquetball once a week with the same guy, and I now say to myself, 'This is my sanctuary.' I'm still a jerk to him on the court, but that's racquetball. At my poker group, I stop and look around the table at the five to fifteen guys and think to myself, 'This is my sanctuary; these are the guys in the lifeboat with me.'"

He often tells the people he leads, "You can create your own community if you don't have one. Find your own practice; here are some examples. Don't shy away from thinking you can't. There are lots of options."

The deep changes necessary to accelerate progress against society's most intractable problems require a unique type of leader—the system leader, a person who catalyzes collective leadership.
—Peter Senge, Hal Hamilton, and John Kania

Building Trust

The quality of trust Patrick has built up in his team is occasionally reflected back to him in affirming ways. At an organization-wide meeting one day with thousands in attendance, the interim CEO was talking about the process of hiring the next CEO. One of Patrick's physician leaders raised her hand and asked the interim CEO a very pointed question that contained within it a criticism of the approach they were going to take.

Patrick described what happened next: "As she sat down from the microphone and he answered it, a woman next to her said, 'That kind of question gets people fired in my part of our organization.' This medical director of mine said, 'Not in Patrick's organization.' When I heard that I thought, 'That's exactly the kind of trust that we are working to create together, so that we aren't passive aggressive. We don't hide things that would be really, critically important for us to know to do our work, to care for our patients better.'"

Patrick told me that he is more mindful of trust now that he's seen how practices like the touchstones—and his own mindset as a leader—can establish and hold safe space. "I'm mindful of just how precious that container is and to be careful that I don't ever ignorantly lose that trust with my people."

Imagine if organizations and institutions were viewed as Möbius strips "writ large." Organizations are often blamed for problems without anyone acknowledging that policies, decisions, systems, and corporate cultures are products of the people inside. Being willing to tackle hard conversations within an organization, to make room for honest debate and differing opinions, is an act of courage that requires and invites integrity. Aligning employees with a higher vision and purpose creates congruence. Alignment is not providing marching orders and directives; alignment is the natural outgrowth of inviting people to bring their best selves to the shared work and taking part in creating and achieving that vision together.

That Patrick brings his authentic self plus the touchstones and poetry into his work is a bold experiment in culture change, and he does so with patience. He knows that a leader's role is to create and nurture trustworthy conditions and to be willing to take part as a learner himself.

How would you describe your workplace culture? What kind of alignment do you experience in organizational life?

Awakening Leaders with Poetry

Leadership is full of moments when our humanity is asked to show up. It's often our internal landscape and weather, which only we see inside ourselves, that make the night-and-day difference for the people around us. One of the best ways to help one another access what we're thinking and feeling is not head on but rather through the side door, through something that is unusual for most leaders and organizations: poetry. Poetry accesses that part of ourselves we don't normally invite into leadership.

Patrick is one of many leaders who told me that poetry has become an important tool for him, both for internal reflection and for connecting with colleagues. Patrick even shared poetry with his patients.

"There were times near the end of my practicing career when I had the courage to offer someone a poem or the like in lieu of a prescription," he told me. "I especially recall a woman going through a messy divorce due to her husband's infidelities and asking about an antidepressant, and I said, 'Actually, what you need is an anti-grief pill, and we don't make those, but this poem by Mary Oliver might be helpful.' (It was 'The Journey.') It opened a whole new level in our dialogue—and saved me from feeling useless in the face of her grief."

Another such leader is Diana Chapman Walsh, president emerita of Wellesley College.[3] Earlier in her career, a retreat experience with Parker Palmer had unleashed her inner poet. When she stepped into her presidency at Wellesley, she invited Parker to come and speak at a multifaith baccalaureate service the evening before the installation. "He read the Mary Oliver poem 'The Summer Day.' It's a beautiful poem that ends with 'Tell me, what is it you plan to do with your one wild and precious life?'" Parker talked about his experience with poetry and then he told Diana, "The world needs presidents who are also poets. Keep your poetry alive."

About two years later, the challenges of the presidency were pressing in on Diana as she climbed a steep learning curve. She arranged to spend a weekend with Parker and his wife, Sharon, at their home in Madison: "One of the first things I said to him when I arrived was, 'Parker, I haven't kept my poetry alive. I just don't have time. There is so much I have to learn. I'm letting you down.' He took that in, and we took a long walk at the end of which he offered, in his gentle way, 'I wonder if you could find it within yourself to think of your presidency as your poetry?'

"This new frame for thinking about the essence of my work was enormously powerful and helpful. There are so many distractions that push us away from our deepest longings and truest insights that we need to be able to find our way back repeatedly, as Parker's offer enabled me to do in that instance."

Poetry helps leaders reconnect their inner and outer lives on the Möbius strip. It becomes a natural leverage point for leaders to slow things down for themselves and others—providing time for personal reflection and at times a communal response. Poet and Courage & Renewal facilitator Judy Brown explained what she has seen in her work with leaders: "Leaders are attracted to poetry for its ability to say what might be in their heart but they don't want to say directly. When we choose to read a particular poem or quote to people, we're offering them something to make sense of themselves, but we're also offering a huge amount of our self, because we're saying implicitly, 'This touched me. This is important to me. I want to read it to you.' It's both an offering freely given, and, on the other hand, it is an acknowledgment of open authenticity about who we are in a world that doesn't necessarily invite that and where it may feel risky sometimes for people to be who they are."

Poetry speaks to a different part of the brain, which helps us move out of our default thought processes through creative disruption. It speaks to our hearts. W.H. Auden famously quipped, "Poetry makes nothing happen." Poet William Ayot says Auden got that seriously wrong: "Poetry gives us direct, unmediated access to the 'invisibles,' those unseen, unspoken qualities of empathy, imagination, and creativity that give our lives both meaning and depth. It lifts us out of our left-brain obsessions with short-term, literal, reductionist results and mechanistic outcomes."[4]

Ayot points out the energy generated by speaking poems aloud: "It feeds both speaker and audience and, at its best, brings a gathering of disparate individuals to one of those deep and reflective communal stillnesses that the Quakers call 'companionable silence.' It's a curious phenomenon."[5]

Patrick's story introduces many concepts identified as important by other leaders inspired by Courage & Renewal concepts and the writings and wisdom of Parker Palmer. As we go on, you'll recognize the same elements—becoming self-aware, building community, finding purpose and meaning by employing the power of poetry or other artful things, and asking good questions and listening, all of which cultivate trustworthy space. These practices for cultivating trust among people can at first seem strange and somehow as mysterious as the Möbius strip. Now that you've seen how one person over time has combined them into his way of leading and living, we'll go more in depth to unpack the concepts and practices so that you can see how they work.

3

Have You Met Your True Self?

There is that in me—I do not know what it is—but I know it is in me.
—Walt Whitman, "Song of Myself"

Ed France still remembers the moment that sparked his passion for the work he does today. He was a young teen, visiting his grandparents who lived in a tiny Mississippi town where the commercial stretch of Main Street was abandoned and insects were louder than traffic noise.

Ed recalls one day when he was tidying up his grandfather's woodshop, a little shed adjacent to the house. It held tools, scrap wood, hardware—seemingly all anyone would need to fix up a house or rebuild almost anything. His granddad had opened it as a retirement business called Dixie Do-Dads, but it was shuttered because the more he aged, the less he was able to work.

"It was a good old tool shop. I remember thinking about how much of a waste it was; all these tools were just kind of sitting there. While this shop sat locked up, neighbors literally a stone's throw away lived in dilapidated structures.

"I came to the realization that given his views and mentality, it would not be possible for him to share his tools with other members in the community, because most of that community was black. I realized as a kid what racism was. There was an established social order that was very entrenched. All the black people in town, they would be called by their first name, where any white person would be called Mr. or Mrs. and their last name. And entering the house, well, unless you worked in the house, black people did not go into white people's houses.

"My realization was really sad. I had this daydream that he would have, in his old age, actually opened up his tool shed for members of the community to come in and borrow tools. The reality was a really sad reality."

Ed told me he didn't understand the unspoken code that prevented neighbors from borrowing, something he thought of as a normal thing. "I remember feeling upset that this discriminatory mentality resulted in squandering a resource instead of offering it up. I hoped that I could act differently, to find a way to do just the opposite, to be inclusive and sharing of resources someday."

Ed's daydream of his grandfather's community tool-lending shop stayed with him. Some years later, he was further inspired by libraries in Oakland and Berkeley, California, that loaned not only books but all kinds of tools, from wheelbarrows and ladders to power tools and gardening implements. He began to imagine possibilities.

"I liked the idea from an efficiency standpoint; I liked the idea of a community toolshed. *That's* the kind of community I wanted to live in: one that shares resources."

Ed took to heart his wish for such a community. He began his career working for the city of Santa Barbara on environmental issues, while on weekends he and a group of friends would lead bike rides and show up places around town with their tools to fix bikes for free. The city is a very expensive place to live, and has a large lower-income working class. He's fully aware of the frequent cultural segregation between Latinos and whites.

"A lot of the folks here don't have access to good bikes or tools or replacement parts. And a lot of these folks rely on bikes for transportation."

So Ed started Bici Centro, a community bicycle workshop and thrift store. Two years later, Bici Centro merged with the all-volunteer Santa Barbara Bicycle Coalition (SBBIKE), a twenty-year-old advocacy group that promotes biking for safe transportation and recreation. Ed became executive director of the new blended agency. But success didn't happen overnight and not without traumatic growing pains. Ed nearly burned out in the process.

What made the merger challenging was the resulting organizational cultural clash between a primarily older group who saw their role as one of advocacy at public meetings versus a younger group who wanted to create community programs. The organization weathered those growing pains, but it still wasn't smooth sailing, and funding was limited. The agency was renting a building that was nearly free but falling apart. That was demoralizing for people, which manifested as a weak volunteer base—tough when you count on volunteers for such labor-intensive services.

"It felt shitty, like the community didn't care. For the first time, I had gotten to the space of being fully cynical, feeling like 'The community has shown it doesn't want this kind of program.' The last few years have proven that isn't true, but that's how I felt, and it was becoming my reality."

Worn out by his discouragement yet devoted to his work, Ed was committed to being present for everything that happened in the organization—and that made for what you might call a divided life. He was on a nightmarish treadmill of chasing goals, taking evening meetings on weekdays, going to events on weekends, and performing ongoing tasks. For six years, Ed did not take time for personal appointments, anything social, or going to classes.

"Basic self-care just didn't happen. Obviously that's not a good thing, because long term you're only cheating the future. My style of operating was to always be there and always be fully responsible. I don't know how my wife stayed with me."

Ed pointed out the social workload on top of all that, wanting to be available to his staff and volunteers. "I didn't want to just get it done. I couldn't just clock out and say, 'All right, you guys, you can close up, I'm out of here.' Anytime you are engaged with people, you find out about their challenges and their struggles, and you want to do something about it, but that's over and above what you're already scheduled to do.

"When you're passionate about your work, that passion can come through like a lightning storm, not like a consistent steady stream of energy you can forecast and use," Ed said. "That fire can make people passionate in a way that is violent. And that passion can preclude people from being thoughtful about what they are trying to do. Ultimately it can make people jaded when others don't share that passion."

Ed's low point coincided with being invited to a local Courage & Renewal program called Courage to Lead for Nonprofit Leaders. Ed admitted it was tough to make time for his own self-care and renewal. "The choice to stop and invest in reflecting is not logical when you're in the middle of the intensity of doing all these things. But reflection time is extremely valuable in every way. It creates a space for emotional intelligence."

Disengaging from work was like literally depressing the clutch, Ed told me. "Suddenly you are liberated for a short time from all those activities you are constantly trying to accomplish. At which point you can reflect not only on those activities but back to your first experiences as a kid or adolescent, or whatever, to ask yourself 'What was the first step that took you in this direction?'" That's how Ed recalled his grandfather's toolshed and his wish that those tools could be shared with the community. Connecting to his daydream about his grandfather's toolshed at the Courage retreat series shifted how Ed brought himself to his leadership. Fueled by that recollected wish, Ed found clarity during the retreat and his vision today is in the spirit of self-determination and social justice.

"I used to joke that I was the head custodian, because that's my style. Now I really see my role as being the person to hold the vision. Before in the exact same situation, the main complaint I had was that people were not coming together around the vision. Now people are coming together a whole lot more around the vision, because I'm allowing myself the space interpersonally, within myself, to be a keeper of the vision. Vision is not a mission statement. Vision is you leading out of your own spirit."

Ed described what that vision looks like at SBBIKE: "We have a shared sense that this is good to be doing, an enjoyable thing. There is a sense of community, there's a sense of purpose. In a concrete sense, we are refurbishing bicycles. That's great. There's recycling, there's bicycling, there's those classic all cliché environmental do-good things.

"For me, I mean, I love bicycling, I love riding my bike. I do it every day. But the vision is *self-determination*—in community. Basically it's like, 'Yes we can,' but it's more of a 'Yes we are.' Together we are creating this.

"It's how I hold myself, what I express, what I show that expresses the vision. I think that's how the world really works. How we live is the vision."

But seldom, if ever, do we ask the "who" question. Who is the self that engages in leadership? How does this self impact the practice of leadership, for good and for bad? How is the self continually honored and renewed as we lead?
—Parker J. Palmer

Knowing the Self Who Leads

The underlying premise of the Courage Way is that we all have a trustworthy source of inner wisdom that informs our lives and leadership. It is our identity and integrity, the sum of our shadows and light, our true self. Without knowing our true self, we cannot be an authentic leader.

Just as Ed came to recognize, leaders must find clarity about what they value, what unique gifts they have to offer, what contribution they wish to make. Strength and resilience as a leader come from knowing the ground on which you stand, the convictions you will act on with courage. But that's not all. Resilience comes from being aware of and accepting your limits and what problems your shadows are causing. That is wholeness—and that comes from knowing your true self.

Otto Scharmer, author of *Theory U,* acknowledges this inner life: "We observe what leaders do. We can observe how they do it, what strategies and processes they deploy. But we can't see the inner place, the source from which people act when, for example, they operate at the highest possible level, or alternatively, when they act without engagement or commitment."[1]

This inner place Scharmer speaks of is more than intellect, ego, emotions, and will. In the inner work of leadership, it is a light behind the eyes, the energy that animates us, or, as Howard Thurman puts it, "the sound of the genuine in you." Instead of *true self* or *soul,* you could say *inner wisdom, essential self,* or even *trusting your gut.* Poets, musicians, and mystics have given words to the essence of who we are—our human spirits—when we take off the trappings of our resumes. John O'Donohue calls it the dignity somewhere in us "that is more gracious than the smallness/that fuels us with fear and force."[2] William Stafford appeals to "a voice, to something shadowy/a remote important region in all who talk."[3]

Although Parker Palmer often refers to his inner teacher, he often says that what you call this core of our humanity doesn't matter, "but *that* we name it matters a great deal. It's important to recognize it: If we don't name it anything, we start to lose the *being* in human being. We start to treat each other like empty vessels or objects to be marketed. When we say 'soul,' or 'identity and integrity,' there is something to make a deep bow to.

There is a word for it in every wisdom tradition."

Beyond being the sum of your life experiences, the true self is a mystery that simply is. How do you get to that underlying mystery of knowing people deep down? Intimacy is not necessarily the goal of every relationship in community, especially in the workplace. But respecting that each person has an essential core self, an undeniable dignity and humanity—now *that* is worthwhile.

I mean the soul simply as shorthand for the seismic core of personhood from which our beliefs, our values, and our actions radiate.
—Maria Popova, literary and cultural critic

How Do You Access True Self?

True self is not defined by your resume, although that may hold some clues. How do you access Popova's "seismic core of personhood"? For some people, the idea of true self (however named) is already part of their lexicon or religious tradition. That wasn't the case for Ed. When he learned to reflect on his leadership path and carve out more time to clear his head, he didn't describe it as caring for true self or soul, but *that he did so* was vital to his leadership. He describes the experience as "inner space exploration."

"There's so much depth within us. Our brains are like a whole space system, a galaxy in and of themselves. Not just the neural connections and the complexity. There is so much to explore just within ourselves, but we generally don't do that, and [self-realization] is almost just a happy by-product. That inner exploration is very useful for leading."

Other leaders agree. One said, "Understanding that every person has an inner teacher radically changed my life. It was powerful to begin viewing each person and myself as creative, resourceful, and whole, and learning to trust and believe in that *first.*" She sees leadership as helping people find that inner source of power and empowerment.

An education leader explained that she recognizes true self by rereading the journals she's kept since she was eighteen, where she can see common threads running through her life: "The themes are the same, the dreams are the same, the core of who I am is the same. I may be of a different age, be in a different job, or live in a different place, but my inner teacher is always there with me reminding me (sometimes less gently than others) of who I am, what I stand for, and whether or not I am being true to my essence."

Some leaders say they can recognize when true self shows up by the way they feel in their body. One woman told me, "It's like connecting to some source. There's an energy and a power to it. And peace. Even if it's scary, it's so certain. It feels like 'This is right.' And it usually happens in public (though sometimes it's happened in my writing) when there's some risk involved. That *full* alignment doesn't happen all that often. That's why it's so amazing when it does. I might feel 75 percent aligned most of the time, but not completely."

It's notable that this leader says that true self appears when risk is involved. That is where true self and courage connect. What if courage is the life force that animates you in moments of decision and action? As this book unfolds, keep an eye out for moments of courage and see if you notice how true self is there, too.

A *good* leader is intensely aware of the interplay of inner shadow and light, lest the act of leadership do more harm than good.
—Parker J. Palmer

The Shadow Side of True Self

It's one thing to focus on the "better angels of our nature," but authentic leadership requires that we acknowledge the whole picture. It's pure physics that we can't have light without shadows.

Marie-Louise von Franz, Carl Jung's closest colleague, says that Jung was once frustrated at people getting caught up in the negative connotation of shadow as the dark, unlit, repressed side of ego, and in exasperation he said, "This is all nonsense! The shadow is simply the whole unconscious." She goes on to explain that the shadow is a "mythological" name for all that is within us that we do not know about.[4]

An excerpt from "An Away-Day with the Shadow" by poet William Ayot helps us see that sometimes shadows are not evil, but may be good intentions gone awry:

Who'd have thought that ill could thrive here and yet it does—in every one of us.

That kind and supportive manager over there is eating her young team: gnawing their bones, sucking out the marrow, destroying their chances with her relentless care and devouring nurture.

That brilliant enthusiast, jumping up and down, with fifteen solutions and a redesign for breakfast is sending his colleagues into spirals of despair, firing off ideas like a Catherine wheel, never allowing any one thing the time it needs to settle or grow.

The mean-lipped man, sitting in the corner, who's been there, done that, seen it fail a thousand times, is poisoning the company he professes to love with his cynical bile and his fear of change.[5]

Ayot's characters are unaware that some internal, unexamined pressure is causing harm to others around them: (1) the supportive manager not trusting someone else's inner resourcefulness; (2) the enthusiast not allowing space for ideas to take life; (3) the mean-lipped cynic not recognizing that change can happen without diminishing one's original contributions.

In addition to the individual shadow, there is the collective shadow, which von Franz points out can be seen in families, organizations, towns, and nations. Shadow is seen in racism, fascism, nationalism, militarism, extremism, and so many "-isms" that reveal the deepest chasms of our collective experience in society. It can be seen in the scapegoat or the black sheep who is forced to carry the shadow of the others. It can be seen in the unhelpful, unhealthy habits and blind spots in organizations, and in areas where transparency is lacking, and such shadows impede progress.

Yet shadows are part of being human, so there must be room in our hearts to see them and reclaim them. If we stay stuck in denial, hate, shame, and blame for our shadows, we cannot heal and grow. We cannot lead in an authentic way.

It's one thing for people to know their shadow, but it's another to express it or integrate it into their lives. Von Franz tells us with compassion, "To have the courage to accept a quality which one does not like in oneself, and which one has chosen to repress for many years, is an act of great courage. But if one does not accept the quality, then it functions behind one's back ... This requires great care and reflection if it is not to have a disturbing effect."[6]

As leaders, we must become aware of how inner dynamics—our shadows—affect the default behaviors that often sabotage our lives. It's usually not until a crisis forces us to take stock, as Ed's burnout did, that we begin to see what's causing the lack of alignment. Once we have met and acknowledged our shadows, we can get back to a place of wholeness—and help others do the same.

The Shadow of Functional Atheism

In *Let Your Life Speak,* Parker writes about five shadow-casting monsters that plague leaders: (1) self-doubt about identity and worth; (2) fear of losing the fight with a hostile, competitive universe; (3) "functional atheism," the belief that ultimate responsibility for everything rests with us; (4) fear of messiness, chaos, dissent, innovation, challenge, and change; and (5) denial of "death," such as when we allow projects and programs to continue that should have been unplugged or when we fear failure rather than reframe failures as learning.[7]

In Ed's case, his working style was like that of many leaders with functional atheism—the unconscious, unexamined conviction that if anything decent is going to happen, we are the ones who must make it happen. It can lead to problems with control, frustration, stress, burnout, and overwork.

"My dad used to say, 'Find something you really enjoy doing and work half days.' Of course, the joke was that a half day is twelve hours, not four. At least he could laugh at his overworking."

When leaders start out as entrepreneurs, for example—the sole person in charge of a project or business—their capacity to "do it all" can create a belief that they *must* do it all, and do it well, by yesterday. Add to that a sense of truly caring about their project as their "baby" and it's hard for them to know where to cut back or let go.

"Understanding what your leadership attributes are, what your inner drive is, allows you to modulate and regulate your passion to achieve what you think you can achieve," Ed said. "That's a really nuanced and deeply centered way of being. I learned that holding the vision doesn't mean I have to schedule out every minute of the day. Overall I've allowed myself the space to work in a way that's vastly better than the work I was doing two years ago. Not that I was working badly; I was working hard."

True Self Offers Empowerment

Because of his own inner work, Ed is now more conscious of how the people he works with bring all of their past and their views into day-to-day happenings. When people question the way things are done, he hears them out, listening deeply without feeling a need to always give advice. He sees this listening as creating both buy-in and empowerment.

"I now trust that it's going to work out. I trust my staff, and if there's a problem, we'll deal with it, debrief about it, and learn about it for the next time, whereas in the past I was not really capable of that in my leadership. Now it's going to work out because we're set up for everyone to be empowered.

"Anybody who engages with us is trying not just to hear the vision or understand the vision; they are trying to make their own stake in the vision."

By sharing his vision more visibly, by embodying his vision, Ed has inspired more engagement from volunteers, board, and donors. As a result, the organization is having an impact in the community.

Within six months of completing the Courage to Lead series, Ed led a successful capital campaign to raise money to buy the building the organization had been renting. He continues to make time for "clearing his head space" to think of new projects, which are as much about his internal passion for social justice and self-determination as about his external goals for bicycling safety and advocacy.

I had a chance to talk to a woman who has worked with Ed for seven years, his education director, Christine Bourgeois. She has witnessed his transformation from the bicyclist with a big idea to the exhausted start-up entrepreneur to the self-assured executive director. When I asked if she knew about his grandfather's toolshed back in Mississippi, she replied, "Ed is a good friend, but I don't know everything about him."

When we reconnect who we are with what we do, it doesn't mean that people around us need to know our whole story. The result of our inner work simply shows up in the courage to lead. Inner work becomes visible in the way we bring ourselves to our outer work, the ways we demonstrate caring for the larger community. Integrity shows.

By choosing integrity, I become more whole, but wholeness does not mean perfection. It means becoming more real by acknowledging the whole of who I am.

—Parker J. Palmer

Trust Your Wholeness

If you don't relate to the idea of true self right now, that's all right. You don't have to believe in the *soul,* per se. Start with the idea that in leadership it helps to recognize and access your inner resources.

Self-awareness starts with understanding that self is more than your outer image, your job title, your identity in relation to others (mother, father, sister, brother, friend, spouse, colleague). True self is fundamentally good, even with its shadows, because it is already whole. True self is your hidden wholeness—it's not always in plain sight but it's there.

Beyond a surface understanding of self is the true self, where you can access your reliable, trustworthy inner guidance. By learning to trust in true self, you grow in self-awareness and create space for others to do so as well.

4

Courage Takes Trust

As we start to really get to know others, as we begin to listen to each other's stories, things begin to change. We begin the movement from exclusion to inclusion, from fear to trust, from closedness to openness, from judgment and prejudice to forgiveness and understanding. It is a movement of the heart.

—Jean Vanier

A physician named Lynne Fiscus was offered a once-in-a-generation opportunity to lead the endeavor to build a new clinic that would consolidate more than thirty individual clinic locations into a single space. She knew the project would be challenging. Although the new building was designed for a more modern and flexible practice, having to build it during the recession meant more clinics in fewer rooms. It would also mean being open longer hours for better patient access. Nobody had a choice about moving. Clinicians and staff were angry, complaining, "Here I am in the academic world where I'm expected to teach and do research and do clinic. Now you're telling me that sometimes I have to have clinic 'til seven o'clock at night!"

On top of all that, Lynne had to deal with three organizations that did not have a history of alignment: the university, the hospital, and the physician practice organization. She had to find a way to bring together people who had been mistrustful of each other. In her first few weeks of being in the position, she held one-on-one meetings with medical directors, clinic managers, and faculty stakeholders and attended many clinical meetings. Her intention in entering these meetings was to hear how these people felt she could be successful. Lynne found herself in many raw conversations about disappointment, anger, and hurt.

"It was really clear to me that my role was not to figure out the optimal room utilization resources at three-thirty in the afternoon of pulmonary clinic. I needed to be the person who could give capacity to people to stay in this work."

Lynne had attended several Courage-based leadership and resilience retreats that her employer had offered for professional development. Lynne also had the mentoring support of another physician. "That really helped me focus on what I wanted to do and actually set me up to be able to take on this large role that I have today." Lynne brought some Courage practices she had learned into the way she led this new building endeavor. One was giving groups a common focal point to begin discussing difficult topics and problems.

"I started each of my monthly meetings with medical directors and clinic managers by introducing poetry. The first few months, people would say, 'What? Someone brought a poem to start off their meeting?' For months I continued to get head scratching and equivocal looks."

"I've been very intentional about how I run meetings. I brought in poems and intentionally reflective activities, Circle of Trust touchstones, examining not just the 'what' of leading but connecting to who we are and how we lead. Doing so made it clear that this wasn't just the same old, same old. I wanted to make sure it felt different than what had happened before. It helped us get out of some of the old patterns of being and patterns of relation we had gotten used to with one another."

One day, Lynne was inspired to use a video in her next meeting about the new building initiative. This meeting was a large one, with seventy people, including medical directors and clinic managers. Lynne introduced the topic of transitions and posed a few questions. Then they all watched a YouTube video called "The Parable of the Trapeze" that includes a voiceover of Danaan Parry's words: "I see another trapeze bar swinging toward me. It's empty and I know, in that place in me that knows, that this new trapeze bar has my name on it. It is my next step, my growth, my aliveness coming to get me."[1]

Lynne explained: "It was just this great metaphor for everything. You know, we're leaving physical space and flying through the air, and it feels out of control. What are our opportunities for learning, for growth?"

The conversation that followed was productive, and completely different from what would have been possible nine months earlier. After the video, Lynne asked the leaders assembled: "If the trapeze artists take risks with the security of a safety net below, where do you find security in the work that seems often overwhelming?" One answer was that they were piloting new things *before* moving into the new building. Another safety net was that the basic work of caring for patients wasn't changing, especially the human connection of comforting patients in distress.

Afterwards, one of Lynne's colleagues said privately to her, "I didn't want to say this in front of the room, but one of the things I feel like makes trapeze artists so successful is they just have ultimate trust in one another. That's part of what's really hard about this work, is that we've still got a big deficit in trust organizationally." This lack of trust had been named in earlier leadership sessions discussing a potential merger in the midst of this project.

Lynne used the same video and reflective process a few more times with different groups. The conversations continued to be generative.

When it came time to open the new building months later, it was decided to control some of the chaos by moving only half the clinics the first week and using reduced patient schedules. Even so, it was rough. A new environmental services vendor hadn't delivered enough trash cans to the building due to a shipping delay. Automatic hand-sanitizer dispensers weren't working due to missing batteries. Individual clinic areas were missing the appropriate sharps containers to dispose of needles, posing a safety risk to patients and employees. The leadership team was meeting twice a day to stay apprised.

After hearing those concerns for two days, Lynne made a tough leadership call. She told her team, "We're not going to open our doors tomorrow until we've gone through and made sure every single room where we're sticking a needle in somebody, we've got somewhere safe to put that needle when we're done with it."

Lynne, along with senior executives from the environmental services company, the construction company team, and the infection prevention team, went room to room making sure there was a sharps container in each one. By midnight, they finally all agreed that it would be safe to take care of patients the next morning.

But then, midafternoon on day three, there was a complete IT network failure. For four hours there were no electronic health records. The land lines didn't work, only cell phones. But the biggest problem was that because it was a brand-new building, every patient needed guidance.

"It was such a dark period of time," said Lynne, "specifically for our leadership team. We were frenzied, harried, running around. I kept thinking, is anything ever going to work in this building again?"

It was supposed to be exciting, this third day of opening a brand-new clinic, but it was not, at least not in a positive way. Amazingly, the staff and patients were fine. Nothing bad happened to any patients when the network was down. Lynne spent the afternoon walking around checking on things, handing out gift cards to patients and chocolate to staff. She was worn out, wondering how she was going to come back for day four.

On top of her leadership role and practice as a primary care doctor a few days a week, Lynne is also a mother of two young children. She had missed multiple nights at home during the clinic's opening days. And she had to fly out of town for business the next day. Her colleagues encouraged Lynne to go home so she could have dinner with her kids. Later, hearing that the IT network was back online, she didn't need to return that night. Alone with her thoughts after putting her kids to bed, she found herself asking, *What is my role as a leader in this time of excitement, chaos, and disappointment?*

Despite how hard she and her team had been working, she realized that she needed to reframe this situation for her team in a way that helped them. "If

I'm wondering how I can go back tomorrow, I know every single person on our leadership team, who's been so invested in this project for so many years, is probably feeling the same thing."

It felt like climbing back up the proverbial trapeze ladder. Lynne went to bed, but couldn't sleep. At five in the morning, she got up and wrote an e-mail to the members of the team who were working in the new building that week:

Team,

As I have been reflecting on the events of the last 3 days, I continue to come back to the "Parable of the Trapeze." We had a discussion months ago what were our safety nets as we "let go" of the old care model, old habits, and old building to fling ourselves forward into our future.

We talked about the safety nets of our staff knowing what to do, how to care for patients, we talked about practicing (your staffs clearly had) and we talked about trust in one another.

We can certainly say that yesterday was a day we needed all of our safety nets.

Trapeze artists don't allow themselves to believe that the use of the net constitutes failure. They must, as we must this morning, climb back up that tall ladder and prepare to do it all again after they fall. Nerves and butterflies are natural, but it is our work. It is what we do. It is who we are.

The trust we have in one another is not that our partners will never disappoint us, will never let us slip, never make mistakes. Nor do we expect that our partners believe that we will get things right 100% of the time. The trust is that ourselves and our partners are as committed to the success of this trapeze endeavor as we are. I have seen that commitment from our physicians, staff, and internal and external partners this week all across the building, and out into the arrival plazas and beyond across all hours of day and night.

We have already heard from our patients what a beautiful thing our care model is when it is working well. Let's dust ourselves off and start climbing that ladder again this morning.

Please know how deeply grateful I am for all of you and couldn't imagine flinging into the future with a better group of partners.

For trapeze artist inspiration, the link is here: https://m.youtube.com /watch?v=HWvV5N4hOGc

Take care and please remember to be good to yourselves and one another.

—Lynne

A month later, Lynne sent out a similar message to the larger group of employees, medical directors, and clinic managers. "I expressed my gratitude to them for their part and explained how we're changing how we lead this organization. Had they not been so honest in our earlier conversation as a group six months earlier, we wouldn't be at this place where we are today, able to help each other through these things. We wouldn't have had the language; we wouldn't have had the trust; we wouldn't have had the conversation. It was, for me, a great moment to be able to step back and say how far we've come from fifteen months ago when I started. I think back to how crazy, crazy those first few days were and how we were able to respond to one another with kindness and understanding in a way that, I hope, will set the tone for how we're going to be in relation to each other in the future."

No one can change the world by a new plan, project or idea. We cannot even change other people by our convictions, stories, advice and proposals, but we can offer a space and ourselves where people are encouraged to disarm themselves, lay aside their occupations and preoccupations, and listen with attention and care to the voices speaking in their own center.
—Henri J.M. Nouwen, theologian

Creating Relational Trust

Developing courage as a leader boils down to trust: trusting yourself, trusting other people, and developing an ability to trust in the balance of life overall. Trust takes time to create, and at the heart of trust is a leader's own self-awareness and social-emotional intelligence. Trust requires listening to one's inner life, which can translate into greater empathy and willingness to invite reflection among colleagues, which can in turn inform a sense of shared purpose and optimism.

Relational trust is a specific form of trust that arises from interpersonal relationships—or social exchanges—*between* people in an organization, community, or network. Contractual trust, however, may be enhanced by good social relationships but it explicitly defines work, products, or services to be delivered with legal ramifications for failure to do so. Most businesses operate on contractual trust without recognizing that relational trust within the corporate culture itself may be the make-or-break key to success.

Many workplaces today function as a social system, or a community, working together around a shared purpose. At their best, there is rapport, cooperation, and belonging, forming a cycle of healthy and productive relationships. Complex problems, competing priorities, family dynamics, and stress-filled, siloed work are just a few factors that contribute to a breakdown in trust.

Relational trust at first glance is simply about trust *between* people: Do I trust you to do your job so that our shared endeavor moves forward? We depend on each other to fulfill the obligations and expectations defined for our roles. That leaves us vulnerable to power asymmetries, to misunderstandings, to breakdowns in communication, to all sorts of tensions that can wreak havoc not only on relationships but also on our individual capacity to handle stress. In fact, relational trust comes from our *inner* perceptions and interpretations of others' behavior and motives. This inner territory is full of potholes and shadows that demand we tend to our own self-awareness.

Tested in Schools

Our framework on relational trust came out of the Center's roots in education. During the same decade that educators and physicians were beginning to experience reflection in community through our Courage to Teach and Courage to Lead retreats, parallel but unrelated research affirmed and advanced the importance of the inner lives of educators. Researchers Anthony Bryk, Barbara Schneider, and colleagues named relational trust "key to advancing improvement in urban public school communities."[2] Even when variables such as poverty, racial isolation, and student transience were factored in, the strong correlation remained between relational trust and student improvement in standardized test scores in reading and mathematics. In schools where trust between teachers was strong, students' test scores improved. But schools whose staffs reported low levels of trust both in 1994 and 1997 had "virtually no chance of showing improvement in either reading or mathematics."[3]

Informed by Bryk and Schneider's research and other more recent studies, in 2012 the Center for Courage & Renewal with researchers from the University of Virginia came together to develop and pilot a program called Leading Together: Building Adult Community in Schools.[4] In schools where Leading Together protocols became integrated into school meetings and culture, the study showed improvements not only in relational trust but also in professional capacity. Teachers reported feeling more inclined to learn and innovate, a greater loyalty and commitment to their school, and a sense of collective responsibility to keep improving their school. All that added to an increased sense of optimism and collective efficacy.[5]

Four Lenses of Relational Trust

Relational trust involves discerning the intentions of others. We observe and interpret the behavior of others through the dynamic interplay of four lenses, often applied unconsciously and simultaneously in default snap judgments. These four lenses, as named by Bryk and Schneider, are respect, regard, competence, and integrity.[6] A severe deficiency in any one can undermine trust. When trust goes missing, we're often unaware of more than a gut feeling. This framework can help us pin down not only what's missing but also what can be done to repair it.

Respect

Respect involves honoring the important role each person plays in the workplace and the mutual dependencies among team members. The quality of conversation, including genuine listening, makes a difference. It's one thing to follow procedures to ensure that each person is heard; it's another to make sure all feel that their opinions are not only heard but valued and will be considered in future actions.

The touchstones are ground rules that increase relational trust because they create a commitment to respectful, nonjudgmental, and meaningful conversations. Whether they are read out loud as a meeting begins, or whether the practices become internalized, the protocols for deeper listening create an intentional way to interact. In our Leading Together pilot study, school teams collectively created their own touchstones or adult community guidelines to provide shared norms that hold the adult community to high standards of professional practice.

The way Lynne held cross-departmental meetings helped people recognize themselves as part of a bigger whole. That set the stage for people to get to know one another beyond their job functions. This latter point weaves in with the next lens, personal regard.

Personal Regard

We often work in a complex web of roles and relationships where power dynamics can't help but exist, leaving people in subordinate positions often feeling vulnerable. When the more "powerful" person makes a conscious commitment to relieve uncertainty or unease, it can create a sense of being cared about. This might entail leaders expressing kind concern about someone's personal life, creating professional development opportunities, or otherwise extending themselves beyond what their leadership role might formally require. In other words, if you make me feel safe in being vulnerable, I'll return the favor.

When Lynne expressed her dismay at missing another dinner with her young kids, her fellow leaders responded by encouraging her to go home. On another day, Lynne was on the other side of the equation. An employee abruptly left a conference call that ran late into the evening. Soon after, he texted Lynne and another physician to apologize: "So sorry. I had to pick up my kids at day care." She texted him right back and said, "Don't apologize. You're talking to two physician moms. Multitasking is our superpower."

Lynne reflected on that interaction: "That's not something people should ever feel like they need to apologize for. It's the reality of our lives these days, and we've got to be able to figure out a way that we can help people do both work and personal life."

Lynne's values around wholeness and work-life balance show up in her personal regard for her team, and that contributes to relational trust in the long run.

Competence

This lens of relational trust involves how people measure leaders' and coworkers' job performance or the value of their contributions. We're not talking about annual performance evaluations between supervisor and employee. In the context of relational trust, we're talking about the many informal observations and judgments—positive and negative—that we make day-to-day about people's apparent capacity to maintain order, to wield fair discipline, or to maintain calm under pressure, for example.

Lynne recalls what went well during those hard days, especially during the network outage. At the infusion clinic, the competent nurses were unfazed. They simply walked across the street to the hospital to print out consent forms.

"They were all in problem-solving mode, focusing on the right work in a way to be able to completely care for our patients. It got me thinking about our safety nets. Because they had practice, they knew what to do. They've been through system outages before in the old building. Not that it happened all the time, but it was just like, 'Oh yeah. Okay. We'll just figure this out.'" Lynne and her leadership team, by contrast, were distressed because there was very little they could do. While IT was working on the technical solutions and care teams were serving patients, the leadership team felt useless.

On the surface, the idea of competence seems to refer to an objective process of assessing roles, responsibilities, obligations, and expectations, but in terms of relational trust, our own shadows affect how we perceive competence. We often judge others without knowing the whole story.

Sometimes we feel blame or shame and project our own darkness onto others. We wonder if anyone knows that we don't have a clue what to do next with all this complexity. Senior leaders interviewed in the report *Thinking the Unthinkable* gave voice to fears of feeling like imposters because of their inability to perform despite being highly paid.[7]

Integrity

When there is consistency between what people say and do, we call that integrity. We say they "walk their talk" or "keep their word." We sense integrity when a person's work appears to be guided by a deeper moral-ethical commitment.

For relational trust to develop and be sustained, Bryk and Schneider note, leaders and followers must be able to make sense of their work together in terms of what they understand as the primary collective purpose: *Why are we really here?*[8] To what higher purpose do we answer besides the obvious bottom lines?

In schools, teachers or principals demonstrate integrity when they act with the best interests of children at heart, especially when they must make tough decisions. Integrity is seen when teachers take a risk in using new instructional methods for the sake of improved student learning or when principals speak out against a central office policy they believe won't help children. Such behaviors affirm that upholding the shared values of the school community comes first.[9]

In health care, integrity translates into making the health, safety, and well-being of patients one's highest priority. Lynne did this when she insisted on the placement of sharps containers in every clinic room necessary. Her leadership team did this by stepping in to ensure that patients were guided throughout the facility when it first opened.

What might integrity look like in business? It's not only the opposite of the immoral and unethical behavior most often reported in the news. Look for circumstances where someone goes the extra mile or goes against the grain. Integrity often requires us to stretch and be stronger than normal. Integrity demands an extra measure of responsibility and resolve to do the right thing. Integrity is refusing to participate in unfair business practices. Resisting pressure to meet quotas that cause harm. Relinquishing a sale or a competition for the sake of winning long-term loyalty. Retracting misinformation.

Integrity requires a shared understanding of your organization's purpose and values, and being committed to living them out. It requires reflecting on how you prioritize decisions for all the bottom lines—people, planet, profit, and purpose—and then clarifying which people you are talking about: your shareholders and board, your employees and their families, your customers? Integrity means releasing a scarcity mindset and redefining short- and long-term value.

Building and maintaining relational trust are daily and lifelong practices that take hard work and heart. With the four lenses of this trust-building framework, leaders of all kinds can become more aware of their own blind spots and see where they can take responsibility for ensuring improvement. Leadership is an opportunity and an obligation to create the conditions in which trust can arise. Courage practices contribute to fortifying trust within, between, and among people.

> You need only claim the events of your life to make yourself yours. When you truly possess all you have been and done ... you are fierce with reality.
> —Florida Scott-Maxwell, playwright and psychologist

The Inner Life of Trust

Trust isn't found or formed in one day, one meeting, one conversation, one e-mail, or one video shared and discussed. It's how we stay in the conversation that matters, especially the difficult ones. Can we let the tensions between us stretch our hearts and minds open? Can we move along the Möbius strip, recognizing how our inner perceptions affect our outer relationships and decisions? Can we make the time, space, and effort to get to know each other without judging? As you'll see in the next chapter, reflecting—alone and together—on the big questions we face can shift the possibilities toward trust. And with trust comes more courage to stay engaged and to lead.

5

Reflection in Community

Our lives as leaders both demand and deserve reflection. They demand reflection because we must know what is in our hearts, lest our leadership do more harm than good. They deserve reflection because it is often challenging to sustain the heart to lead.
—Parker J. Palmer

A speech pathologist named Rosalie "Rosie" Martin can help adults who've never been able to read because she can break the task down into its tiniest components. That allows the learner to be successful at every point of the process. Rosie explained: "I say the word 'spoon,' and it's just this little collection of sounds: s-p-oo-n. Four sounds, five letters but four sounds. That little sound pattern is an auditory symbol that represents that thing. It's not that thing; it's the symbol that represents it. All of language is our symbolic system for representing the world."

"To me it just feels like my daily work, but I have realized that other people find it amazing." That's the most true of the people she helps. A prison inmate we'll call Peter (not his real name) finally learned to read and write at age fifty-one thanks to Rosie. As soon as the inmates are able to write, Rosie asks them to reflect. In his own written words at age fifty-three, Peter describes the difference Rosie made in his life: "It's funny, before I went in I didn't know reading and writing, but deep down I must have known how to, but I didn't know how to start before Rosie showed me I could do it. Rosie somehow opened the door and let the man out who would write. I knew there was somebody at home up there, but he didn't want to come out to play. Now he's out and he just can't stop writing."[1]

Rosie has been a speech pathologist for thirty years, but teaching prison inmates took some courage. Rosie first opened her business as a sole practitioner while her children were young, and now is the busy owner and director of a high-profile private speech pathology clinic. The main clinic in Hobart also supports three outreach clinics in outlying areas of Tasmania.

For years, Rosie had been thinking about offering her clinical skills to nearby Risdon Prison, where she knew that many adult inmates could not read or write. Very often they've come from situations where they've experienced repeated failures. They might have tried to learn to read when they were in school, and often they tried again in various adult literacy programs. They would need specialist interventions to make real and sustained progress in acquiring literacy skills. Yet Rosie was reluctant and, in some ways, afraid to extend her services further. It wasn't fear of the inmates or of being inside a prison. Something deeper, unnamed yet, was holding her back.

One day, Rosie was sitting in an auditorium listening to a plea for volunteers to work at literacy tasks with prisoners. A colleague was also there, across the room. When the event ended, they walked toward each other.

"We knew simply what the other was thinking. We know how to add quality [of intervention] for these complicated souls unable to respond to regular methods of learning to read. We have the skills. We ought to be sharing this knowledge with these vulnerable men and women."

But something more than her intellect was recognizing an opportunity. Rosie wrote about what that felt like: "In the moment my eyes met hers, I felt in my depths a breathless sparkle like bright flow between river stones—vivacious élan which I have come to recognize as my herald of heart action."[2]

Her aha moment provided momentum, but Rosie still needed nudging. Two days later, she met with a career coach for the second time, who said, "You will always try and get all the details lined up before you do anything. Why not just go and get started?"

Rosie realized what else had been holding her back: "I desired to bring my skills into a wider social justice setting, but I knew that I didn't really know how to proceed." Rosie ran her clinic business well, but she knew little about running a charity and engaging with the bureaucracy of a prison system. "Also, I felt the responsibility of ensuring that the clinic didn't wobble too much if I withdrew my time to work in the charity—I have employees who depend upon their jobs." Rosie recognized that her worry was about the organizational shift, not at all about the clinical work. "The clinical work is my area of practiced expertise—I'm completely fearless in that domain!"

The word *chutzpah* was on Rosie's mind, working its way into her heart. Rosie had been pondering the paradox of humility and chutzpah. She recalled different times in her speech pathology career when she had chutzpah. "I am audacious about asking for mentors. I just e-mail and ask. I think they are often amazed—if they are UK or US based—to receive a request from what seems like an exotic place on the other side of the world, and they nearly all say yes. I live my life on the you'll-never-know-unless-you-ask principle."

"The coach's words made me realize I had to jump and trust my cape!" Rosie overcame that mixture of dissonance, desire, and the flurry of confusions that accompany not knowing how to make a shift yet feeling compelled to do so.

"That afternoon, I rang the prison and said, 'This is what I know how to do. Can I come talk to you?' They said, 'Yes, come in and tell us.' So I did, and I got such an incredible reception. Then everything just started to open up."

Rosie began volunteering at the prison several times a week. She founded a charity called Chatter Matters as the vehicle by which to run what became a small pilot project, Just Sentences. Rosie's pioneering work[3] with prisoners uses reflective dialogue practices that come from a clinical intervention program based on parent-child attachment theory.[4] "The Courage Work brought a new depth of understanding to what trust actually deeply means and the depth of trust that needs to be established. I am now more aware of the fragility of trust and the importance of deeply honoring the other person." She trained more speech therapists and prison volunteers, including her husband, Rich, to work with a small number of inmates for the pilot phase. As they started seeing rapid improvement in the inmates' literacy skills, Rosie kept spreading the word further to gain more funding.

"I'd talk with anybody who would listen about what we were doing. I was actively, intentionally making connections in order to share the value of this work and the importance of it, because my skills are as a clinician.

"And then I just realized, actually, I'm not afraid to talk to anybody anymore. I don't feel like I'm scared anymore. I can see that that's been a gradual change in me over the last few years. Chutzpah is a great word. I feel like I've got it."

"When we know and understand ourselves, we can be more honest with our inner selves in a richer way. That provides us with opportunity to be able to bring all of ourselves to the communication, which then opens a space for the other person's communication to be lifted and enlarged as well."

"Am I going to continue to do the thing I was trained for, on which I base my claims to technical rigor and academic respectability? Or am I going to work on the problems—ill formed, vague, and messy—that I have discovered to be real around here?" Depending on how people make this choice, their lives unfold differently.
—Donald Schön

Reflective Practice and the Courage Way

Being a wise and skilled leader is not something you arrive at one day, fully formed and complete. It takes ongoing personal and professional growth that has a purpose beyond one's individual success. Your growth as a leader benefits the people you serve, the causes you care for, and the purpose behind your profit and product.

Reflective practice is at the heart of the capacity to grow as a leader.

Where do you observe your own reflection? In a mirror? In the glass of a storefront you pass by on the street? In the watery depths of a still pond? In the eyes of another person?

We must engage in reflection if we are to see ourselves clearly (that is, become self-aware). By definition, reflection is a two-way process that requires some form of mirror. Reflection can also mean individual contemplation, meditation, or pondering.

Reflective practice is not exactly the same as introspection, which you might call soul-searching or self-examination. In Courage Work it is both an individual and a communal practice. Reflective practice is more than taking time to think about process, learnings, or data. It can be about all of that, yet it's also about checking in with your inner life and doing so with other people.

Rosie's story illustrates why personal growth from reflection is both personal and communal. She was reflective when she recognized her need for the chutzpah to act. Her coach helped her reflect on her tendency to procrastinate until all details are neatly lined up. When she and her colleague locked eyes and realized that they needed to act, that was also a moment of reflecting a common purpose and inclination. Reflection helped her remember other times she had courage. Reflection in these instances may look incidental, yet Rosie is practiced at paying attention to the clues of her life. The real power is revealed when reflection is intentional.

We have much to learn from within, but it is easy to get lost in the labyrinth of the inner life. We have much to learn from others, but it is easy to get lost in the confusion of the crowd. So we need solitude and community simultaneously; what we learn in one mode can check and balance what we learn in the other.

—Parker J. Palmer

Reflective Practice in Community

To become your authentic whole self, you need other people to help you see yourself clearly. As noted in chapter

1, the Courage Way presents a specialized meaning of community as "solitudes alone together" as well as a "community of inquiry."

The poet Rainer Maria Rilke writes of "a love that consists in this, that two solitudes protect and border and salute each other."[5] Parker Palmer expands on how we can support another person's growth: "We stand with simple attentiveness at the borders of their solitude—trusting that they have within themselves whatever resources they need and that our attentiveness can help bring those resources into play."[6]

The word *love* isn't often used in terms of leadership. Not to be confused with romantic love or even intimacy, love can describe the patience required of a good leader who aims to bring out the best in other people. The Center's work is grounded in a core value of love, by which we mean the capacity to extend ourselves for the sake of another person's growth. Working in community stretches people to understand, respect, and support each other, which is why learning to love is one of the most demanding disciplines one can choose. When regarded with love, we are surrounded by "a charged force field that makes us want to grow from the inside out—a force field that is safe enough to take the risks and endure the failures that growth requires."[7]

Solitudes...

Solitude starts with you and your thoughts, along with your journal and pen. If you're truly averse to handwriting on paper, you can choose to keep track of your thoughts using an electronic device. But consider unplugging for a time and see if your heart speaks more clearly when you involve your fingers and hands differently (especially if you're always plugged in for your day job or doing a lot of texting). It's also a chance to draw and doodle. Handwriting is good for your brain, stimulating creativity and relaxation.[8]

Solitudes become "alone together" when you take time to share your reflections out loud with one or more other people. We use the terms *dyads* and *triads* when we invite people to find a partner or two. You can do this in person, in small groups at work, even over the phone with one to three other people who commit to a recurring weekly or monthly peer support call. The protocol is that each person has the same number of minutes to speak without interruption, then it's the next person's turn. You do not comment or share insights on what the person just said. Say thank you and then take your turn. This allows one person to be "heard into speech"—to be witnessed expressing a newfound clarity of innermost thoughts. It's astounding what a difference you can make by doing something as simple as listening without commentary. If time allows at the end, you can ask people if they are open to a question (but if they say no, don't force your opinion). Any speaker can opt to invite thoughts.

Communities of Inquiry

Solo reflection is a form of inquiry, but the reciprocal asking of questions yields an abundance of insight.

Communities of inquiry are meant to support personal and professional growth. Also known as a community of practice, it is where you feel safe enough to be your genuine self and willing to be gracefully challenged by others' open, honest questions and reflection that will help you become more authentic.

Our touchstones define a shared fierce commitment to hold safe space, which creates a communal experience of respect and regard. Done well with intention, such community can generate individual insights and also create interpersonal trust, empathy, compassion, and joy. Yes, even joy—and happiness and celebration.

Community and leadership are required for facing serious, hard issues, as well as mourning our losses and taking stock of our learnings. But they're also about ensuring we have moments of laughter and light—making sure we celebrate accomplishments and take time out for fun.

These pictures [by Cézanne] demanded one's participation, not just one's understanding; a process

that left no room for the distance of detached observation and comparison.
—Heinrich Wiegand Petzet, art historian

Finding Common Ground with Third Things

Engaging in reflective practice with other people, particularly around inner-life questions that draw on our spiritual side, can be tricky when living and working in mostly secular settings. Even in daily life, simply getting to know one another beyond small talk is hard.

In Courage Work, we introduce material that we often call a "third thing"—something to focus on that can help people find common ground. Adding a third point takes us from a polarized stance of two points with a tense line between them and instead makes a triangle. This creates a space, a field, in which to interact and relate.

In *The Courage to Teach,* Parker Palmer says that communities are held together not only by personal power but by what the poet Rainer Maria Rilke calls "the grace of great things." Interacting with such great things helps us discover deeper truth.

The "thing" could be a poem, a teaching story from a wisdom tradition, a case study from your profession, a quote, or a piece of music or art, like the video of the trapeze artists that Lynne used (see chapter 4). One facilitator told me she has a photo of several horses standing in a corral—but the gate is open, and beyond it is a huge open field. She asks people to reflect: *Why are the horses all in a corral when the gate is open?* Just about anything can spark a metaphor to speak to our human condition. As we seek to explore the meaning and significance of third things, we are lifted out of our objective mindset and into a different cognitive space.

The gracious, hospitable power of these third things becomes like another person in the room, a welcoming, inviting, evocative person with whom we're in dialogue and with whom we're learning. Interacting with this third thing as if it were a living being—entering into dialogue with it, getting inside it and letting it get inside us—evokes new insights. We feel safe talking about the subject at hand because we're coming at it from a different angle.

In the Just Sentences literacy program, Rosie brings in essays written by adults who learned to read and write after a lifetime of illiteracy, physical impairment, or brain injury. Rosie partnered with *Island* magazine to publish a collection of those essays. These essays function as "great things" because they speak candidly about the shame of growing up unable to read or write, being bullied, being the bully, being unable to fill out employment applications, and experiencing the triumphs of finally learning to read. In her introduction to the essay collection, Rosie describes what happens: "I have been asking the new learners I work with to read the *Island* essays to me, or I read them aloud to them. I sit across the table from men and women and see eyes well and throats choke as they read or listen. For in honest language, their own hidden pain is gently spoken. And the same soft syllables carry inspiration for who they are and what can be."[9]

Reflective Leadership

Different points in your day or goals on your leadership path call for different types of reflective practice. *Leading from within* requires a capacity to reflect on your own professional practice. *Leading together* requires reflection about relationships and the community context in which you work. *Leading for impact* asks you to reflect on yesterday's learnings so that you can adjust today's actions to keep you moving toward your goals. *Leading for transformation* requires a depth and breadth of inquiry—within individuals, between colleagues, and among stakeholders—so that each person involved finds intrinsic motivation to take responsibility for actions that contribute toward realization of a shared vision.[10]

In the midst of our current environment where there is so much change, complexity, and uncertainty, it's easy to lose touch with what is most important. Many leaders struggle with such questions as *How can I possibly achieve all that is required of me and of my organization? How can I reduce uncertainty and know that the strategies I'm following will produce positive results?* Seldom, however, do leaders ask the questions, *Who am I in this role? How can I be renewed as I work with and relate to others? How can I discover my strengths and work toward common purpose?* Yet these more personal and reflective questions are the key to leading for the long term. Results, challenges, and pressures come and go, but the capacity to reflect on the subject of your work, on your own performance and practices of leadership, and on the relationships you have with those you lead and serve and report to is central to good leadership. Through reflection, you can learn to examine your assumptions and biases, and to contemplate "failures" so that you can learn from them and apply those insights in other situations. Reflective practice isn't just an act of will or the result of encouragement. It has to become a habitual response, a part of everyday life.

> People, even more than things, have to be restored, renewed, revived, reclaimed, and redeemed; never throw out anyone.
> —Audrey Hepburn

Reflection and Renewal

Reflection can liberate us from our inner prison where our shadows and unexamined assumptions, or our simple lack of attention, obscures the clarity of truth. Rosie saw the power of being a reflection partner for the inmates of Risdon Prison: "Suddenly somebody's talking to them like they're an incredibly valuable human being and that they're courageous. They've never thought about themselves in those terms before. They've never thought about the inner vulnerabilities and shame they're holding with not being able to read. They've never thought about addressing that as a point of bravery or of courage."

One of the gifts of reflection is that we get to both listen and be listened to. Reflecting aloud in a trustworthy space generates a sense of personal voice and agency. When leaders feel renewed in terms of "who I am and why I'm here," that renewal can ripple out to rejuvenate the vision, mission, and vitality of their colleagues and organizations. Parker Palmer reminds us that we needn't do it alone: "And yet it remains possible for us, young and old alike, to find our voices, learn how to use them, and know the satisfaction that comes from contributing to positive change—if we have the support of a community."[11]

6

The Courage to Care for True Self

Self-care is never a selfish act—it is simply good stewardship of the only gift I have, the gift I was put on earth to offer others. Anytime we can listen to true self, and give it the care it requires, we do so not only for ourselves but for the many lives we touch.
—Parker J. Palmer

In 2008, Dr. Mukta Panda was chair of the department of medicine at a nine-hundred-bed university hospital. She had just received an award for her dedication to teaching new doctors and her talent for creating innovative and effective residency programs.[1] But Mukta wasn't happy.

"I was questioning my purpose, value, and worth. Two days earlier, I received news about a personal loss of twenty-five years. I was not sure of where I belonged."

She was struggling personally and professionally. The politics and expectations of the department chair role no longer seemed aligned with Mukta's values and gifts. When she had first taken on the role eight years earlier, it was with the goals of growing the faculty team, both in size and in their sense of collaboration, and nurturing young doctors. Over time, the role had come to demand more focus on fiscal issues, less on relationship. "And that's not who I am," she said.

Mukta explained: "The health care system today is very challenging. From every side there is change. As an educator and physician, I'm asked not just to take care of patients but to guide the future doctors. This challenge requires not just technical skills but my full human capacity, to connect that role with my soul."

Burnout can happen to anyone at any time. Conditions are ripe in professions where you face intense competition, long hours, expectations of stoicism, and stigma around asking for help with emotional stress. And that can lead to depression, addictions, physical symptoms of stress, loss of meaning and purpose, and even suicidal thoughts.[2]

Even as she was working hard to help young physicians avoid burnout, Mukta had to tend to her own well-being. One of her first decisions was to accept an invitation to attend a Courage & Renewal retreat offered to the physician award winners.

Looking forward to the weekend retreat on her calendar gave her hope. Then the retreat itself was a pivotal moment. She saw how reflective practices with the support of community could draw forth one's insights. She stayed up late into the night asking herself new kinds of questions: *Where do I belong now? Who am I?*

"Before the retreat, I did not have language or skills and did not know the art of how to have that conversation with myself. I tried but couldn't get past the superficiality of what I was facing. It gave me a really different way to get past the layers of shame, blame, anger, and feeling totally unvalued."

"It was surprising and energizing to remind myself of what I had written about in my medical school application, the reasons I wanted to be in a health profession, to be a doctor. I reconnected with who I am."

Mukta realized that how we perceive ourselves and take care of ourselves is related to so many factors: How do we face challenges at work every day? How do others perceive whether we're knowledgeable or not? How do we cope with negative or positive stimuli? She began thinking more about the link between self-awareness and resilience.

"The key is realizing you have to take care of yourself *and* know who you are. You must have an authentic voice to be able to take care of others—including colleague care, too."

She also realized that the isolation of being department chair, especially given the changing focus on fiscal issues, was depleting her joy in medicine. Eventually she chose to step down and become assistant dean of medical education instead, where she could use her gifts to nurture the well-being of new physicians. She had fresh ideas about how to do so.

Mukta began holding weekly reflective sessions with two colleagues and soon also a resident who they knew was struggling. "I used the third things and reflection process with them. It was truly a circle of trust with the touchstones and confidentiality around it," she said. It wasn't long before they decided to offer the same sessions to their resident physicians. Medical students and residents enter their training with intense altruism and a commitment to care for their patients. But during training, they rarely have an opportunity to reflect on their emotional experiences.

To address this lack, Mukta created a program called Relaxing, Rejuvenating, Rejoicing in Residency sessions (RRRnR). For an hour each Thursday, they gather, without an agenda, and sit in a circle. A few moments of silence allow them to become fully present and to leave the rest of their lives behind. Mukta tells them, "If you have things to do, write them on a paper and tear it up.

Now be present here in this room for the next thirty minutes of your life."

People can bring a book chapter, a video—anything they want to share. The session is a safe space for residents to talk about the emotional experience of being a doctor. "You can talk your heart out, about inherent fears and apprehensions," as one resident described it. Another said, "Dr. Panda's demeanor has such a sense of openness to it, you're not afraid to share anything. We share our deepest fears and concerns, and surprisingly you find answers to questions you didn't know existed."

Now nurses, pharmacy students, and others from all different divisions within the hospital come to the sessions. People get to hear everybody's frustrations and can relate to each other with more empathy. It has created a sense of community that leads to further collaborations and more camaraderie in their work together. People feel that they have a bond, a connection with each other, due to what has been shared in the RRRnR sessions.

In a research project Mukta conducted with a clinical psychologist, they studied the coping skills of residents who had gone through her RRRnR sessions over eighteen months. Residents who attended at least three sessions per quarter had positive coping skills and reported lower levels of stress.[3]

A Ripple Effect of Renewal

One of those residents who benefited from the RRRnR sessions—and Mukta's firm but nurturing guidance—was Ramya Embar. She recalls being often on the verge of burnout during her residency and fellowship. "When I first came to the US, I was in tears because Dr. Panda set very high expectations for me, probably because I was so immature at the time. In residency I was crying about the long hours." She remembers complaining to Mukta, "This work is not taking me anywhere. I don't know why I'm doing this." Mukta would ask Ramya questions to get her back on track, such as *What is your purpose?* Ramya would recall how when she was younger, she spent a few months working alongside her grandmother at Mother Theresa's Mission of Charity in India. Seeing sick people through recovery or being with people who passed away made Ramya want to become a physician. Her parents encouraged her to pursue her dream.

"When you're on the verge of burnout, you have all these thoughts," said Ramya. "I wasn't looking for answers but the right questions. I kept a diary."

At one point when Ramya was feeling especially stressed, she started a daily practice of writing down one nice thing her mother had taught her. She would read through her notebook on hard days. "I'd look for meaning in all those things, as a reminder to keep going."

Mukta also taught Ramya to recover from stress by building in a daily cycle of replenishing activities as simple as taking time to eat lunch or talking to a colleague or mentor. Another way to build resilience is by finding ways to successfully detach psychologically and physically from work for at least a short time. For instance, Ramya copes by doing things that have nothing to do with medicine: "I go to a spot by the river to my favorite tree. I just sit there and listen to music. And I teach Sanskrit classes on Monday evenings."

Ramya benefited not only from restorative activities but also through mentoring relationships. She had the support of elder physicians who kindly received her 3a.m. calls if she needed advice on a case. That helped her overcome feelings of isolation and offered her an ongoing dialogue to make meaning of her professional experiences in the context of her whole life. Mentoring also was a path to paying attention to her own emotions, becoming increasingly mindful.

"Dr. Panda taught me how to have a heart-to-heart talk with my patients," Ramya said. "That phrase can be misleading. We use our minds to talk to one another about things that affect our hearts, our emotions, and feelings. She helped me uncover my feelings and helped me communicate with my patients."

Being more present with her patients brings her joy. "I love laughing with them and building rapport. Patients often feel rushed. But many tell me, 'Doctor, thank you so much for talking to me. None of my other doctors have time to explain things.'"

By slowing down and paying attention to her own interior condition, Ramya is able to recover and show up for her patients. She is taking care of her true self, and that translates into better care for others.

There is a pervasive form of modern violence to which the idealist fighting for peace by non-violent methods most easily succumbs: activism and overwork.
—Thomas Merton

Confessions of an Overactive Writer

Ramya's resilience inspired me to dig deeper into the distinction between self-care and care of true self. The words of another leader I interviewed have stayed with me: "We can't be creative if we're exhausted." As I got close to finishing this book, I was working extra-long days, nights, and weekends to keep my commitments to deadlines. I say that creativity is my caffeine, but I was waking up in the middle of too many nights with ideas I had to write down. My body was reacting with adrenaline surges and crashes. I tried acupuncture, deep breathing, quitting coffee, thyroid tests. I even went for an EKG to rule out heart trouble. Thankfully, all tests showed that I was healthy and strong, in technical terms. A couple weeks later, I submitted the first draft just past noon and breathed a huge sigh! Everyone said, go take a nap! It was too noisy and broad daylight to sleep. Instead, I decided to go for a walk and take my Canon camera along. It had been almost nine months since I'd allowed myself to go play photographer, or play much at all. As I stepped outside, I noticed the weight of my camera in my left hand. I felt the weight of the zoom lens. And I felt a weight lifted as I recognized, *Oh, there I am.* That was the moment I could feel in my body what we mean by true self. A little while later, I sat in the sun and spoke by phone to my son, grown up and living on the opposite coast, starting a new soul-fitting job. Laughing with him, more true self showed up. I am also a mom.

Self-care may seem at first glance to mean care of our physical bodies. It's important to replenish our energy with restorative activities that serve us deep down. It's important to make time for the things—and the people—we love most, so that we can replenish the wellsprings of our passion for living. And that is care of true self. Our well-being depends on tending our wholeness—and not waiting until the end of big projects to do so. Carving out moments to connect with true self doesn't have to eat up time. That connection can feed us instead.

Thomas Merton writes, "To allow oneself to be carried away by a multitude of conflicting concerns, to surrender to too many demands, to commit oneself to too many projects, to want to help everyone in everything is to succumb to violence. The frenzy of the activist neutralizes his work for peace. It destroys the fruitfulness of her own work, because it kills the root of inner wisdom which makes work fruitful."[4]

What's most vital is to care for *true self*, the integrity of who we are at our core. We care for true self when we listen to our emotions, our fears, those things we rarely speak out loud. By asking the right questions of ourselves about the underlying reasons for our soul-deep exhaustion, we can replenish our hearts for the ever-present challenges of being human. That is how we build our resilience. Listening inwardly for those clues is an ongoing practice, not a one-time event. Self-awareness can grow when we make time for reflection. And it helps to have access to the nonjudgmental support of other people.

I must wrap my life around this question: "How do I stay close to the passions and commitments that took me into this work—challenging myself, my colleagues, and my institution to keep faith with this profession's deepest values?"

—Parker J. Palmer

A Creative Response to Suffering

Vera is a longtime, valued top-level manager at a community foundation, where she is committed to excellence in her work with clients and coworkers. When her chronic autoimmune illness began to flare up periodically, she found she had to take a day here and there to stay home and take care of her symptoms. She often didn't mention her condition to anyone, which left her feeling alone as well as ill. When she finally had the courage to bring it up with her managers, they were receptive and helpful in ensuring that their short-term disability policy was updated to accommodate people with episodic "flare-up" health conditions.

However, even with the support of her employer and its "intermittent leave policy," Vera found that her health condition was still difficult to manage, especially during busy and stressful times. She wondered if taking an extended leave from work would help her body heal and enable her to better manage her condition. She also had a growing desire to spend more time with her mother, who was retired, and wanted to travel with her children.

"When my father died a few years ago, my mother said to me and my siblings, 'I don't want you to wait to visit me when I'm sick in a hospital or at my tombstone. I want to spend time with you while I'm alive." Vera began to think about taking an "adult gap year" or sabbatical to include traveling with her mother to Antarctica—the last continent that her mother had yet to visit. She thought of going with her mother to visit the remaining twenty US states left on her bucket list. To have the luxury of time (and money) to travel with her mother and give herself a much-needed break from the daily stresses of work seemed like a worthy yet unattainable goal.

Knowing that time for rest and renewal would be good for Vera, in 2013 Vera's supervisor recommended that she participate in a Courage to Lead retreat series. Over eighteen months, Vera gained skills in reflection and the support of a compassionate community of peer leaders. She finally felt safe enough to be completely vulnerable about her health needs and how torn she was about devotion to work and her physical limits. She shared her desires and plans for her sabbatical with her small leadership circle and closest colleagues, who listened and encouraged her to speak up for her needs. They encouraged her to take care of herself first in order to sustain her commitment to public and community service over time.

Because Vera gained clarity about her core values and her need for self-care, she managed her personal finances to allow for a yearlong sabbatical in 2017. Her participation in the retreat series and a series of peer coaching sessions helped Vera move forward. She created a succession and sabbatical plan to be an experience that would feed her soul and provide rejuvenation for the next phase of her career. Vera was been able to be transparent, focused, and trustworthy with her employer about her plan, and it all started with the courage to tend to her care of true self. She gave her employer a year's notice before leaving and worked with her colleagues to ensure a smooth wind-down of several initiatives she had managed. Vera also helped recruit candidates to serve as her successor.

Vera was living into Parker Palmer's proposal that leaders "must uncover, examine, and debunk the myth that organizations are external to and constrain us, as if they possessed powers that render us helpless—an assumption that is largely unconscious and wholly untrue."[5] Coming from a place of strength and courage, Vera not only practiced self-care but made sure that others would benefit from the systemic change that was needed to establish a policy for intermittent leave. And she worked creatively with her employer to take her gap year in a way that didn't cause problems. But care of true self is more than taking time off. It's living a life that's aligned inside and out.

Care of true self, and sometimes systemic change, are possible when a leader speaks her truth and when another leader listens and responds, truly valuing the well-being of all employees. Vera was fortunate that she worked somewhere where the leadership was willing to be flexible and was open to creative win-win solutions.

> The deeper our faith, the more doubt we must endure; the deeper our hope, the more prone we are to despair; the deeper our love, the more pain its loss will bring: these are a few of the paradoxes we must hold as human beings. If we refuse to hold them in hopes of living without doubt, despair, and pain, we also find ourselves living without faith, hope, and love.
> —Parker J. Palmer

The Ongoing Need for Renewal

What does it feel like when you're in need of self-care? What words do you use to describe your hard days? *Discouraged, burned out, exhausted, demoralized.* Those words don't sound very whole; they sound fragmented and disjointed, just like you feel. It's hard to bring your best self and whole heart to your work and the people you serve when you're frazzled and fried. Renewal is important.

Resilience arises from the self-awareness, care of true self, and meaning-making that comes from reflection—especially reflection practiced within a community that can support you to take your next action with integrity. You discover not only stamina but a renewed sense of purpose for the long haul. Knowing what work is yours to do can give you joy and recharge your inner batteries. But batteries can recharge only so many times before they need to be replaced.

Care of true self is an ongoing task, a way of living. We often wait until something breaks rather than give ourselves a more preventive type of care. For you to live a conscious and most rewarding life, a practice of renewal must become habit. Having a community where you can be completely open and safe is a key way to continually fortify and renew yourself.

Where can you be yourself? Who are your people you can talk with honestly? Can you meet on a regular basis with the sole function of supporting one another's lives? Find a place to be listened to deeply and asked good questions, whether in a therapist relationship or at church or in other ways. Look for places where it's possible.

It's helpful to understand your own story, what got you here, the scars you carry, and what sustains you. When you recognize true self with tenderness, you can attend to what is unresolved. When you know what you're feeling and what is happening internally, you can learn from it, process it, and find your way through life with more courage.

7

The Courage to Answer Your Calling

Everything that happens to you is your teacher. The secret is to learn to sit at the feet of your own life and be taught by it.
—Polly Berends, writer and sculptor

Jonathan Zeichner grew up in a middle-class community in suburban Connecticut. When he was twelve, his parents divorced, and he moved to a tough inner-city neighborhood in New Haven. At his middle school, it wasn't uncommon for students to carry guns and knives and to fight with teachers. As the one Jewish kid in a school where only 10 percent of the students were white, Jonathan at times had to protect himself.

"I learned not be a victim or a target. I had to stand up for myself. I had to develop some bravado."

Jonathan also had to learn how to do more than survive. "I realized early on that certain shared interests transcended class and race. Art. Music. Movies. Pop culture."

After high school, Jonathan moved to the Bay Area and later to Los Angeles to pursue a career as a writer and director for theater and the screen. With every move, Jonathan faced the challenge of how to provide for his eldest brother, who was suffering from schizophrenia and living between the streets, hospitals, and jail. Jonathan had long been a lifeline for his brother, a go-between with the rest of their family—and sometimes his brother's anchor to reality itself.

"Adam would follow me whenever I moved, and I often struggled with the feeling that I was abandoning him when I decided to relocate. It wasn't easy, but I ultimately came to the conclusion that restricting my pursuit of life and work was not good for anybody."

In 1989, Jonathan was in Los Angeles, working in the entertainment business, when he learned about and got involved with an organization doing theater work in psychiatric and homeless settings. The work allowed him to have an impact on young people and adults who shared his brother's struggles. "Once again, I saw how the arts transcended the differences that so often divide people—class, language, background, all those 'us and them-isms.'"

"In 1992, when the Rodney King beating verdicts came down, the civil unrest was devastating. As I sat across town and watched it all unfold on television, what caught my eye most was the kids," Jonathan said. "They were being swept into this wave of anger and indignation for actions and a history that they had no hand in creating. I saw a need for a creative outlet for young people who needed healthier, more empowering and productive ways to express themselves, other than violence."

With a group of like-minded people, Jonathan helped start The School Project in 1993, which ultimately spawned a new nonprofit agency called Inside Out Community Arts, which Jonathan cofounded with a friend and fellow teaching artist-actor. Over the following ten years, Jonathan continued writing and directing, but he gradually divested of his entertainment industry career and began to focus mostly on running Inside Out. After sixteen years there, he was invited to take on the task of turning around a similar but struggling nonprofit in South Central Los Angeles that provided after-school education, arts, counseling, athletics, nutrition, and college scholarships for youth and families facing poverty and great adversity.

A Place Called Home (APCH) was struggling, not only because of outdated facilities and a lack of funding but also because its staff was beleaguered and morale was very low. Decisions were being made behind closed doors by well-meaning board members and lead staff, but the staff culture had become one of mistrust and discontent.

When Jonathan was approached to take on the executive director role for APCH, he knew that this was a do-or-die moment for the organization. He also knew that if he accepted the challenge, he had to do everything possible to succeed.

"I took some time to accept the calling, and I did a lot of meditation and consultation. I went to APCH often over three months to explore the organization inside and out and determine how it matched up with where I was as a person and a leader. In the end, like with any relationship, once all the data is in, you have to go with your gut. I decided to jump in."

Jonathan describes his path as organic, but imperative. "I've always done things that called out to me and that were right for my developmental phase—even the mistakes I've made have been mostly humbling and instructive when that's what I needed. I've never considered taking on a job that wasn't an expression of my values or to satisfy some curiosity. And usually I learn a lot—not always the easy way—and then apply it in the next setting.

"In accepting the appointment at A Place Called Home, I was definitely leaving the known and heading into the unknown. I knew something different would be needed from me as a leader. Without tending the wounds, the needs, and the fears of the staff, execution of the mission couldn't take place in a strong, authentic, healthy way. The board and staff needed to have their hope rekindled." Jonathan knew he needed to grow as a leader to meet these new challenges.

"For years I had the idea that leading meant I had to project a certain kind of energy that was a combination of vision, control, and striding out in front with a banner leading the charge. It was liberating and affirming to realize, from my time in reflection, that what my staff most needed was not for me to put on an act of leadership, but to actually be myself."

"I've been on my own since I was sixteen years old, figuring out life without adult role models. I'm used to making things up as I go along, and willing things to happen. The Courage Work created something more constant inside, an inner sanctum that I have learned to draw from and depend on." He realized that he could shift his leadership to embrace all aspects of his life, what might be thought of as his true self. He could call on his willingness to be foolish, to humble himself, to experiment and fail, to try things and have them not work out.

"It was all experimental to begin with, because I hadn't done this particular turnaround thing before. I set about fixing things and going down to bedrock to give the most battered staff new faith, hope, and trust in the value of the work and in the organization's ability to get to a new, better place."

Jonathan said that earlier in his career, he was playing an aspect of himself, a role, as the leader. "Now I can still be large and in charge when I need to be, and there are times when that's appropriate, but fewer and fewer. Mostly, I just show up as I am, and that allows others to grow and lead, too."

Vocation at its deepest level is, "This is something I can't not do, for reasons I'm unable to explain to anyone else and don't fully understand myself but that are nonetheless compelling."
—Parker J. Palmer

Listening for the Voice of Vocation

As Jonathan discovered, courageous leadership is based in bringing your full self to your work. We need as many people as possible addressing the world's challenges with compassionate, creative thinking, so we need people committed to discovering their gifts and becoming aware of their shadows. We need leaders who are committed to showing up, sleeves rolled up, to apply themselves for the long haul. If it's going to be hard—and it often is—then it helps when leaders can tap into a sense of meaning and purpose, heartaches and joy.

The typical way of seeking meaningful work—or vocation—is to figure out how to match your strengths with possible work or professions. Countless books and processes exist for identifying your personality, strengths, and interests to help you discover whether you are aiming for work that will be a good fit. That's valid and valuable, but it is only part of what is needed.

The word *vocation* is rooted in the Latin for "voice." Finding your vocation, then, first asks that you listen to the voice of your life. This is not the voices telling you what you should do to achieve success, or the ones telling you to follow in somebody's footsteps or to satisfy harsh inner critics. It is not the voice of your ego demanding with grim determination that you make your life something it's not.

In *Let Your Life Speak,* Parker Palmer writes, "Vocation does not mean a goal that I pursue. It means a calling that I hear. Before I can tell my life what I want to do with it, I must listen to my life telling me who I am."[1]

Have you ever noticed how life itself is informing you and inviting you to show up, whether the work is what you had planned or not? Listening to your life speak—*all* of your life, through heartaches and mistakes, as well as your joys—can help you find the clarity and courage to bring your true self to your life's work.

This isn't about showing up as your work self or best self. It's about showing up as your *whole* self. Showing up fully as a leader is not limited to bringing the parts you think are expected, demanded, or acceptable.

We invite you to reconnect who you are (your soul) with what you do (your role). Note that we say *reconnect,* not connect. Our assumption is that deep inside everyone is a true self that knows itself well. Other voices, authority figures, circumstances, and fears can cause you to hide or forget many aspects of your essential core self, but those aspects do not have to remain hidden or lost. Vocation is not a function of external expectations or aptitude or talent. Vocation is an inner sense of what your life is asking you to do, which is to reconnect your soul and role. You might say that a "calling" is your life speaking, and vocation is your response to that call with your choice of work. (Have you ever heard of the call-and-response style of music? Examples include old-time gospels, "My Generation" by The Who, and "I'll Take You There" by the Staple Singers.)

Leaders like Jonathan don't reconnect soul and role by following a set of instructions. They do so over time as they integrate their sense of self—their whole self—into their work. Vocation doesn't have to mean doing one job or type of work for the rest of your life. Some leaders purposely set foot on the path of vocation, predisposed to seek meaningful work; others say they never thought of their work as a calling but more like "a special project for now."

There is no passion to be found playing small—in settling for a life that is less than the one you are capable of living.

—Nelson Mandela

The Meaning of Calling

How do you define the word *calling* as it relates to your career? Do you approach your career or other areas of your life as a calling? When researchers Bryan Dik and Ryan Duffy asked people these questions, they found that as many as 68 percent resonate with the concept of calling, although with two different views.[2] "Neoclassical" callings are experienced or perceived as coming from an external source, named as God, something spiritual, a need in society, destiny or fate, or a family legacy. By contrast, "modern" callings arise from within and are tied to ideas of individual happiness and self-actualization. Both views emphasize a sense of personal "fit" with a job and include altruistic motives to make the world a better place.

Jonathan observed, "Just about everyone I know who has been called to service work for others or for the planet is also working on healing themselves and discovering their value as a human being. I'm no different. I didn't find this work; it found me, and it allows me to feel blessed and useful every day."

Researchers notice that people who identify with their work as a calling view it in several ways: as craftsmanship ("doing work well"), as serving ("doing good work"), and as kinship ("doing work with others").[3] It doesn't have to be just one of these. Each view can inform the others. How do you view your work? When have you noticed that the seasons of your life or different situations call for different views to take precedence? It seems that no matter how you define it, a calling arises from within your heart when you recognize the clues of your life.

In order to discover how life informs you and invites you to the work that is right for you, it's vital to understand how to listen to "the voice of vocation." How have you paid attention to those clues from your life? And how have you answered with your chosen work?

> Start with a big, fat lump in your throat, start with a profound sense of wrong, a deep homesickness, or a crazy lovesickness, and run with it.

—Debbie Millman, educator and designer

Finding Your Voice in Hard Choices

One approach to discovering a sense of vocation is through the back door known as *via negativa,* the way of emptying, shadows, and suffering. Rather than viewing only your strengths or interests, you examine what your limits and heartaches are telling you about where you are meant to be. People often discover their right work by realizing where they are *not* meant to be or by noting how they are *not* showing up, how they are holding themselves back.

Sometimes we hold ourselves back because we feel the tug of hopeless obligation to tend to another's concerns over our own. Trying to live someone else's life, living up to others' expectations or our own false expectations keeps us from realizing our wholeness, from doing what we are meant to do.

Finding and living into our vocation require courage because these choices are often neither simple nor without costs. It's risky to leave what we know, even when the known is unhealthy. It's risky to step into the unknown. Have you ever feared not being welcome, not being good enough, not having the answers? Anytime we are feeling conflicted and fearful, we hide who we are and refuse (consciously or unconsciously) to give our gifts where they're needed. We may fear being punished somehow; being shamed, rejected, dismissed; being unheard or devalued. So we make the choice to play it safe.

Finding the voice of our courageous true self often comes at the moment when we reach a turning point and choose to finally fear not. When we choose to make the hard choices, to take a stand, to show up, to be seen and heard, to walk away so that we can move forward—these are moments when our lives speak out loud. Moments when we decide to step into more leadership responsibility are also moments we answer our calling. Moments when we claim our own life arise from courageous choices of free will that put us on the path of our calling.

We may not feel the hearty embrace of our new life right away, but if we look close enough, we may notice ourselves breathing more freely, sleeping more deeply, and walking with a different heft in our step. Our next work awaits.

> Don't ask yourself what the world needs, ask yourself what makes you come alive, and then go do it. Because what the world needs is people who have come alive.
>
> —Howard Thurman

Finding Your Voice Leads to Creative Courage

The capacity to risk stepping into the unknown is seeded deeply in the rich soil of vocation. Leaders cultivate their capacity to risk by building trust in themselves and in others over time. By embracing the paradoxes of limits and strengths, leaders expand the boundaries of how much they are willing to risk showing up as themselves to grow into the next stage of life and leadership.

"People find innovative responses to impossible situations not because they are well-trained professionals or particularly gifted," writes John Paul

Lederach in his book *The Moral Imagination.*[4] "Innovative responses arise because this is their context, their place. The essence of the response is not found so much in what they do but in who they are and how they see themselves in relationship with others. They speak with their lives." Lederach goes on to say that what he calls the "journey toward change" requires vulnerability and a willingness to risk.

Jonathan's cultivation of his willingness to look inward honestly and to risk being himself with his staff parallels the mission of A Place Called Home. He sees the paradox of strength and vulnerability and how it informs courage. "Kids who grow up in South Central LA and neighborhoods like this are streetwise and have evolved in certain ways, but they are undeveloped and naïve in others. Then there are sophisticated, successful people who are making things happen in the world, but they're fearful and out of touch with their values. Whatever your ecosystem, courage shows up in how you respond to opportunities to go outside of what you know."

Jonathan recalls taking a group of kids to photograph the neighborhood, walking over a bridge spanning the 110 Freeway. One boy just stood there looking down at the traffic, staring and staring, while the other kids were moving along. Jonathan finally went back and asked him, "What's going on?" Still watching the cars speeding by and without looking up, the boy said, "Where are they going?"

Jonathan has never forgotten that moment when that boy's life called him from the freeway. "It was such a powerful moment of epiphany for him to realize that a whole world existed beyond his own neighborhood and experience."

Jonathan likes a Rumi couplet that says, "Be afraid, but don't move the way fear makes you move." He explained why: "I used to think courage was about being fearless. Now I understand that it's not about denying my fear—there are a lot of things to dread in the world these days. But we can develop ourselves to be able to choose how we're going to respond to those feelings.

"That's huge for everybody, but especially our kids, our staff, and our constituents in this neighborhood. There are so many opportunities to get into trouble, to be drawn into tempting and unhealthy dynamics, and to self-destruct. To recognize that one can feel all kinds of ways and at the end of the day choose how to move rather than become a victim ... that's real courage."

True leadership comes not from the sound of a commanding voice but from the nudging of an inner voice—from our own realization that the time has come to go beyond dreaming to doing.
—Madeline Albright

Giving Voice to Courage

What we've also seen over twenty-five years of our work, and what we have seen in the history of social change movements, is that reconnecting who we are with what we do has benefits for the common good. It's as if by finding one's voice, it becomes

imperative to then give voice to those without voice. Courage Work is in service of something beyond the individual self, but it takes renewal of individuals before there can be positive change and growth in organizations, communities, or institutions.

Courage principles and practices, and a supportive community, give leaders the language to speak about their experience, affirm their intuitive leanings that they are on the right path, and help them see more clearly which way to go. In some cases, the way forward is to step into more responsibility or to lead with more voice. In other cases, leaders realize that they are in the wrong place or are ready to grow or need a course correction; they step out of one role to bring their voices to leading somewhere else, either in the same organization or somewhere entirely new.

When we reconnect who we are with what we do, we build the foundation for relational trust, which creates the kind of community where we can engage in greater collaboration and create greater collective impact. At each of those steps, we must tune in as life calls us so that we can answer with courage.

8

The Courage to Question and Listen

A strong community helps people develop a sense of true self, for only in community can the self exercise and fulfill its nature: giving and taking, listening and speaking, being and doing.
—Parker J. Palmer

Greg Sunter is used to being at the front of the room in control of delivering content—first as a classroom teacher, then in school leadership, and now as an education consultant in Brisbane, Australia. Greg no longer thinks of *controlling* presentations. Rather than showing up as an expert, Greg now asks, "How do I *invite* other people into a conversation rather than me leading it?" He does it with questions.

This was Greg's mindset when he was hired to address a toxic staff culture at a primary school. Morale was at an all-time low, and relationships were frayed after a complete turnover in the school's leadership chain within two years. The administrators told Greg that they didn't expect him to fix all the problems in a day and a half, but they needed to start the detoxification process.

Greg met the whole staff—teachers and support staff—at a conference venue for two days of live-in professional learning. All professional learning of the last few years had been conducted on-site, so the opportunity to spend time together in a nice location was much appreciated. The room was set up with circular banquet tables.

After the group spent time in individual and group reflection exploring their current sense of vocation and purpose, Greg posed three questions to the staff: *What is it that as a staff community you want to stop doing? What do you want to continue doing? What do you want to start doing?* Greg had no idea what the staff would say, nor were the questions merely a technique to open the door to his own already formulated solutions or programs. He genuinely wanted to know what these negative, disgruntled people would say about their lives together.

The staff began by reflecting and writing individually about the questions for about thirty minutes, then took turns sharing insights with their table group for another half hour. Greg then asked people from each table to share aloud with the entire group.

At the first table, someone said, "We need to stop backstabbing each other and all the negative talk that goes on in the group." The next group reported nearly the same: "Like the first table, we really need to stop all the bitching and all the complaining that goes on."

By the time half the groups had reported, they were overdue for lunch, and the venue manager was standing in the doorway expectantly. Greg acknowledged the man, but wasn't going to interrupt what was happening. The group was hanging attentively on the words of each person who shared the group responses.

"It wasn't my agenda to get instant consensus," Greg said, "but I think they were waiting for somebody to ask the question, 'What do you want to stop happening in the staff?' Every group named it. That was significant. There was something of a collective sigh that went through the group; they'd finally said it out loud to one another. The deputy principal came up to me as we broke for lunch, and he said, 'You've just earned your money.'"

That day's conversation was simply the start. The toxicity wouldn't improve overnight, but having everyone answer the same questions created a shared self-awareness that opened the door to listening and thus to the possibility of trust. Estranged and negative colleagues began to listen to one another and to focus on questions that were vital to everyone.

In his consulting practice, Greg is often asked to facilitate a day focused on community building. What he tells his clients now is, "The biggest thing you can do to improve community is to build trust. The number one way to do that is to listen to each other, to actually talk to each other, share something of yourself, hear other people

share something of themselves. Let's work first on trust so you can actually then have conversations about other things that need to change."

Greg told me, "Courage practices build leaders who can pause and reflect before charging into something, who can realize that they don't necessarily have all the answers. They can ask open, honest questions to elicit what others are thinking and then value their responses as genuine contributions. That's pretty powerful in leadership and not valued in the world. You're supposed to be decisive. You're supposed to be out front leading, not asking what others think, but that's what good leadership looks like."

The process of asking open, honest questions and listening to another person reflect aloud—whether in a retreat, in the workplace, or in daily life—is a powerful form of companionship and transformation. As people are heard in a nonjudgmental way, then affirmed and accepted as they realize their shortcomings and successes, they become more comfortable. The reciprocity of conversation creates relational trust and fortifies people to risk showing up and speaking up. It also elicits the best from them, which benefits the organization and everyone in it. Higher-quality questions and listening make for better organizations and positive impacts on results.

> "Good listening"—like "trust" or "wholeness" or "authenticity"—are things that emerge because we are disciplined stewards of the structure that we're creating.
>
> —Judy Brown, from an interview with the author

What Is an Open, Honest Question?

Most of us would acknowledge the value of asking questions as part of a trustworthy and productive conversation, but asking open, honest questions is an art. It requires the listener to set aside preconceptions and instead tap into a deep and generous care for the other person. In fact, the primary characteristic of a well-crafted open, honest question is that you couldn't possibly predict the answer. You ask because you genuinely want to know and because you are trying to engage others in order to gain understanding and demonstrate real listening.

These additional guidelines help ensure that questions are truly open and honest:

- Avoid questions with yes-no or right-wrong answers.
- Make questions brief, straightforward, and to the point. Avoid preludes or rationales that would allow you to insert your own opinions or advice.
- Use the other person's language to frame questions and avoid injecting your own interpretations or projections. *What did you mean when you said you felt sad?* is an open, honest question. "Didn't you also feel angry?" is not.
- Ask questions aimed at helping the person explore his or her concern rather than satisfying your own curiosity.

The purpose of open, honest questions is to take us beyond the typical patterns of conversation to a place of inquiry and discernment. They promote exploration and authenticity, rather than jumping to conclusions or defaulting to our own assumptions. Open, honest questions help other people gain self-awareness and clarity to inform their course of action.

The best questions come out of deep listening. When you're in a conversation with somebody who's struggling with something, try to think of it like this: *What's a question I could ask right now that is, to the best of my ability, in service of this other person and what he or she is struggling with?*

Ideally, a good question incorporates language that speakers have used, which demonstrates listening but also often encourages deeper exploration of a theme or image they used. Try to pay attention more to the moment, rather than starting to predict the next thing you expect might come up.

I asked leaders to tell me the best open, honest question they ever received. One answer especially stayed with me. Marcy Jackson, cofounder and senior fellow of the Center for Courage

& Renewal, said: "One of the questions I have loved and that has stopped me in my tracks is this one: *What makes your heart sing?* It's a very simple question. It has pulled me back from my sometimes overserious nature or trying to think everything through, rather than paying attention to what brings me joy."

When we learn how to listen more deeply to others, we can listen more deeply to ourselves.
—Parker J. Palmer

The Gift of Listening Without Fixing

A senior management leader we'll call Bob had tension with another person on staff, which made him feel as though his value to the organization was being questioned. He went to the CEO, Mike, for advice—and to vent a bit, too. He paced around the corner office, unsettled. Rather than give Bob instructions about what to do next, Mike consciously opted to ask open, honest questions. That meant asking questions

Mike couldn't possibly know the answer to but that would help Bob listen to his own inner wisdom.

In their conversation that day, Mike posed these questions in response to Bob's unfolding story: *What does that mean to you: feeling your value is being questioned? How does that feel to you? Do you recall a time when you had a similar feeling? How did that turn out? What are some things that occur to you as a next step?*

The questions helped Bob connect the current situation with some other times in his current life and in his past. He was able to look at the workplace episode differently, and he gained a new perspective on how to approach his colleague for further conversation.

Mike's internal stance as a leader was the foundation of this curiosity-driven yet nonjudgmental conversation that led to Bob's insights. What Bob couldn't see was that Mike was also embodying a few other touchstones to create safe and trustworthy space: *allowing silence, turning to wonder,* and *no fixing, saving, advising, or correcting.* This approach empowers others to make wise decisions based on their own genuine inner knowing, rather than just accepting a superior's advice (or seeming to but without a sense of ownership). Mike said, "I'm fascinated every time in these interchanges how much more satisfying the result seems to be when I don't jump in with the first advice that comes to mind. My conversation with Bob had so much more texture to it. My impression was that Bob appreciated the fact that I didn't dive in and tell him what to do and that I was interested enough in the situation to help him talk through it."

Mike knew that his approach was atypical. "Allowing silence is challenging, especially in the workplace. People are taught to fill the silence. If you engage in conversation with open, honest questions and you give people time to ponder, that means you have to be patient with the silence."

Mike sees how this form of conversation supports a workplace culture of compassion and empathy. "It's harder to stop and think of asking an open, honest question. But it is a form of caring for someone, and it comes across that way—as caring." It also communicates a charged expectation that Bob will address the situation responsibly and will be accountable for maintaining professional relationships with colleagues. This is paradox in action, to hold the tension between caring and accountability.

Mike told me that learning to ask open, honest questions is both a challenge and benefit of Courage Way practice because it's made him a much better listener. "I've realized there is no greater gift you can give someone than deeply listening to them." Open, honest questions are a form of humility in leadership, too. It's easier but can be a form of arrogance to ask questions that try to manipulate people into the answer you want them to find.

> An open question leads us to what Einstein referred to as a "holy curiosity."
> —Dawna Markova

Open, Honest Questions and the Möbius Strip

"An open question is a choice point, the twist in the Möbius strip," writes Dawna Markova, in an essay for the book *Living the Questions.*[1] She has us imagine ourselves on the Möbius strip to experience the interplay of the inner and outer life (see chapter 2). "To achieve mastery we are taught to answer questions that are asked. This leads us to the outside of the strip."

She alludes to the advice of Rilke to the young poet that some questions cannot be answered on the spot but must be lived into over time. She continues: "An open question takes us to the mystery of our inner world, where patterns and meaning unfold like petals. An open question leads us to what Einstein referred to as a 'holy curiosity': a curiosity that is nourishment itself without the pressure of having to constantly fulfill our appetite for explanations and solutions." In the story of Bob and Mike, we see Mike's capacity to realize in the moment that he could choose to ask open, honest questions. By making that choice, Mike is aligning with his own values, remembering the kind of culture he wants to create, one where people feel valued. Mike knows it may appear inefficient and ineffective to spend time listening when he could quickly give advice and move on to the next thing on his list. But by listening carefully and offering questions, he's making it safe for Bob to be vulnerable *and* to find his own direction. With patient listening and wholehearted inquiry, Mike models how to have a generative conversation, and it's possible that the kind of questions he posed will inspire Bob to consider asking such questions with his colleagues in the future.

In the process of being listened to and prompted with good questions, Bob was *fortified* in these ways: he was able to remain calm while he reviewed past experiences that were similar, and to reimagine possible ways to respond; he found the courage to have a difficult conversation, despite not knowing how he might be received; he then resolved to repair the tension with the other employee in a follow-up conversation. This wholehearted process helped Bob become more resilient because he found his own resourcefulness.

All of this happened because Mike decided it was important for him as a leader to make time to listen; to ask open, honest questions; and to refrain from giving quick advice, even though this is not the course leaders are usually supposed to follow: "We're all taught to be problem solvers, especially if your title is CEO or manager or VP. We condition people to come to us for answers. Sometimes there are easy, concise answers; usually the things that aren't very important. We're conditioned to believe that we're doing our best work when we're solving things for people. But things that are most important to people don't have clear, easy answers—or else they would have already acted on them."

Mike had an interesting insight about other benefits of taking a more open-ended approach, especially because it is outside of the expectations for leaders: "I've tried to swim against that current and force myself, especially in dicier personal issues, to ask open, honest questions. I've noticed that first, people really appreciate that you don't think you're smarter than they are, as if you can fix their problems and they can't. Second, people appreciate that you're willing to take the time to let them talk through an issue and even, in a sense, create the context for themselves by having to explain it.

"It's a luminous experience when it rolls out, but it takes fighting through that initial crust of 'How do I fix this for this person and move on to the next thing?'"

Open, Honest Questions in Daily Life

Mike has found the practice of listening with open, honest questions to be invaluable at home, too. As a husband and also a late baby boomer, Mike describes himself as "a protector" who is inclined to give advice. A few years ago, his wife retired and took a part-time leadership job with a nonprofit, but within a few months realized that it wasn't a good fit. The organization seemed to desire a bookkeeper and office manager more than a strategic visioner to lead growth. She loved the mission and the people, but she was limited to administrative duties. She didn't need the job for the income, but she naturally felt some misgivings about leaving so soon after starting.

Mike's wife shared her feelings over coffee at their kitchen counter, their conversation unfolding over many weekend mornings. Because her expressions of frustration were interspersed with asking his advice on functional management questions about accounting or record keeping or by-laws, Mike was in tricky territory. He wanted to be helpful to her inner executive but also empowering to her inner leader to discover her truth.

"My inclination would have been to say 'You don't owe them anything, here's a date to tell them you're quitting,'" Mike said, adding that he would have offered an advice-filled program of what to do, when to do it, and how not to feel bad about it. It would have been easy to get it over with a quick decision. He said, "It was giving me grief because it bothered her!"

Instead, Mike asked his wife, *Why do you feel the way you do? What would it look like if it were working better for you and for them than it does now? How would you know when it was time to make a decision about whether to stay or not stay in the job?*

He concluded, "The questions honored that what she was going through was complicated, evoking emotions and issues of integrity that needed some space and needed to be recognized. None of which would have happened if I'd said 'Can that thing!'"

Mike and even the biggest fans of the open, honest question approach know that such questions are not appropriate in every situation. They are best employed when it's important to create safe space for the other person's inner wisdom to flourish. Sometimes people just want feedback and information. Family members have been reported to say, "Can you ask me those open, honest questions to help me figure this out?" Yet sometimes they get impatient and say, "No, I'm really asking for your input right now."

At the end of six months, Mike's wife did resign from her position as executive director. But because she had taken time to reflect, rather than bail out in frustration leaving the agency in a lurch, she created a congenial, understanding transition. She helped the nonprofit find a replacement. "She left under good circumstances, with no remaining bad feelings," Mike said. "It was as positive an experience as you could make it."

It's hard to transcend a combative question. But it's hard to resist a generous question. We all have it in us to formulate questions that invite honesty, dignity, and revelation. There is something redemptive and life-giving about asking better questions.

—Krista Tippett

A Practical Application—Performance Reviews

For many people, performance reviews seem like rather soulless exercises driven by organizational imperatives. Designed to measure performance in order to determine whether employees have met their goals and thus have contributed to the organization's results, they are usually highly structured, formulaic, and data oriented. Unless a leader or manager consciously sets out to make the performance review process about more than numbers, it's not likely to help employees grow or gain greater insight into themselves and their work. Being rated on accomplishments is necessary, of course, but it is only part of the picture. If you want to invite people to bring their full and best selves to work, you must engage in a different sort of conversation.

Greg Eaton decided he wanted to change the way performance evaluations were held in his company, a thriving business that organized corporate meetings and incentive trips. The company was known for providing exceptional customer service.

"Whether in universities or business, in all my years I saw the same thing. If the manager said good things, people just humbly hung their heads or maybe smiled. And if there was a growing edge, you could literally feel the tension in the room because of who was speaking. Whether the evaluation was good or bad, it just shut down engagement and conversation."

So instead of rating employees on specific competencies at his company, Greg invited his managers to list each employee's strengths and potential for growth. Before the performance discussion, they also asked employees to reflect on two questions: *What is it that you're most proud of? What was a challenge or a struggle?*

The new process changed the relationship between manager and employee. Hard topics still had to be addressed, but giving employees time to reflect in advance and to start the conversation with what they were proud of made a big difference.

Greg said, "Most people had never been asked what they were proud of before, and it made a few people get teary eyed. Those were moments to celebrate. I saw people make huge gains in their work competence and performance and pride because they were taking more ownership."

At the Center for Courage & Renewal, annual reviews are similarly structured with open, honest questions that each employee receives a few weeks ahead of time. The supervisor and the employee reflect in advance, then go out to lunch to chat, taking turns sharing "lauds, learnings, and looking forward."

Lauds: *What has gone really well that we might celebrate?*

Learnings: *What has been learned in the process? How do we "take stock" of where things are now compared to where we thought they might be?*

Looking forward: *What are you most excited about in this coming year? What concerns you* *most? What ongoing professional development will help you to grow in your current job and for your future? How can I be of most help to you and your work?*

The manager then writes up their joint discussion and gives the employee a chance to make changes before they finalize it and put the document into the files to use as a baseline for next time. The process builds trust that is fostered with almost weekly check-ins that create a sense of ongoing conversation. It's a give-and-take of openness, of being invited to say what's really true.

Building Trust with Open, Honest Questions

Open, honest questions build trust in groups and teams by encouraging listening for the sake of understanding the perspectives and stories of others. Such questions can lead to shared insights and generate a sense of cohesion even when there are individual differences. That's what Greg Sunter was doing when he asked the school staff what they wanted to stop doing, continue doing, and start doing. The group stood together on common ground as they envisioned a new way forward out of the negativity that had been plaguing them. Open, honest questions are also an excellent way to fully include and reflect the interests of all stakeholders in organizational outcomes, objectives, and plans. They make dialogue more productive and help group members suspend their tendency to analyze, critique, and give advice.

Open, honest questions can also be used more informally to start building trust in regular staff meetings. For instance, a team could be invited to respond to this question: *What is one thing that was really great last week, or didn't work last week?* Or you can ask questions that get people talking about their lives in ways they normally wouldn't at work, such as *How did your family celebrate birthdays?*

More organizations are turning to human resource processes that explicitly focus on the professional growth of employees. Some are known as deliberately developmental organizations

(DDOs), as featured in Kegan and Lahey's *An Everyone Culture.*[2] Frederic Laloux writes of similar organizations (including the Center for Courage & Renewal) in his book *Reinventing Organizations.*[3] The process of asking open, honest questions cultivates a learning culture, and that is good business. In his book *Curious,* Ian Leslie contends that curiosity may be society's most valuable asset.[4] A society that values order above all else will seek to suppress curiosity, but one that values progress and innovation will cultivate it. Healthy curiosity is important not just for problem solving but also for cultivating empathy. In Courage Work, the curiosity of open, honest questions goes further to cultivate self-knowledge and access to inner resourcefulness.

As you do the outer work of a leader, it's necessary to do your inner work, too. Open, honest questions get to the heart of what matters by inviting true self to speak up with real answers. People you trust who are able to pose good questions and truly listen can fortify you—and others—in hard times. Just as you can cultivate the capacity to ask good questions and be an empathetic listener, you can also cultivate the types of relationships (especially in community) where this quality of interaction is welcome and practiced. Asking such questions—combined with the other practices around listening—is integral to making wise decisions in any aspect of life.

9

The Courage to Hold Tension in Life-Giving Ways

We engage in creative tension-holding every day in every dimension of our lives, seeking and finding patches of common ground. We do it with our partners, our children, and our friends as we work to keep our relationships healthy and whole. We do it in the workplace—in nonprofits and business and industry—as we come together to solve practical problems.
—Parker J. Palmer

As the only female manager in her department of a metropolitan county government, Jill Boone was in charge of janitorial, landscaping, and sustainability services. That meant, in part, that she had to supervise union workers who had had a difficult history with the person in the manager's role before Jill.

Jill knew that her predecessor had not been well liked, but now the union reps' accounts of his tyrannical behavior revealed how bad it had been and how it had damaged relations between management and staff. Her open, honest questions allowed her to understand the situation and opened a space for her to speak from her heart and share her hopes that together they could create a workplace that would be respectful of everyone.

"I'm really new to this," she said to the union group. "I've never managed in a union environment. But I don't see any reason why we can't talk things through. Why are we at odds when we are basically on the same side?"

Jill also extended an invitation to regard her in a fresh light: "I may do something that you really disagree with. It may be really stupid. What you have to understand is, I may not know. It's not like I'm intentionally out to get you; it's that I probably don't know any better. Just come tell me; just let me know."

Her humble stance took them off guard. They were more used to the confrontational power play voiced as "Look, I'm management and you're not." Within the first six months, the confrontational attitudes dissipated; relations between the union and her department were measurably improved, and stayed that way during Jill's tenure.

"That invitation to come and talk to me instead of going to upper management really made a big difference. They educated me, and I was really open to being educated. If you're speaking from your heart, then people open up to you more. They're willing to have that conversation with you, because they recognize that you're not speaking from a point of manipulation or a point of power."

Jill recognized that each person's inner resources should be acknowledged, honored, and cultivated. Besides asking open, honest questions, Jill was intentional about applying the "no fixing" touchstone as much as possible and encouraged her supervisors to come up with solutions to their problems.

"The deep listening without judgment is what really opens your heart to people who are different than you. Also, not thinking you have to have the answers for everybody else is important. As you move up the org chart, or the hierarchy in work, you assume—and people assume—that you're above them for some reason, because you know more than they do. The reality is you really don't. Sometimes you have to take everything into consideration and make a hard decision, but it's good to have the humility to understand that you don't necessarily know better. Just because you're the manager doesn't mean that you know everything. You don't *have* to know everything. Going into it with that humility is really helpful."

Transforming Conflict, Not Managing It

Jill told me one story about how she had to discipline a union janitor who was mouthing off and having issues with his supervisor. Before being reassigned to the job he now had, he had cleaned

Jill's office area, so they had gotten to know one another. They had often talked and joked in a friendly way. This new problem with his attitude didn't seem in keeping with the man she knew. When the problem was brought to her attention, Jill invited the janitor to sit down with her for a conversation. She asked him questions about what he was going through so that she could find out what was really underneath all of this sudden uncharacteristic behavior.

"By being open to him as an individual, and being open to the fact that maybe we made a mistake, maybe something had happened, we found the answer. At the union meeting where people could choose their position by hierarchy, he had selected a position that involved being in a different building every day, and getting new instructions every day was driving him nuts. He didn't like it at all."

As it turned out, the janitor could be reassigned to a new position in one building, despite initial resistance from the union, which Jill resolved by having another meeting to talk things through. But she also told him he needed to clean up his act: "Come see me and say hi, but don't get sent here because you need to be talked to."

Jill's leadership and her willingness to listen and to capitalize on a relationship she had already built enabled her to orchestrate this tense situation and other win-win outcomes because she began with recognizing wholeness in people.

"I still had to be the disciplinarian, and sometimes I had to fire people, but I wanted to be able to understand that people are basically good. If you come from the heart, to a large extent, people are willing to have that conversation."

There is a tension between the duties of management and the aspirations of leadership. Conflict is unavoidable and must be dealt with. But awareness of your own and others' internal landscape—being present to emotions in the moment, being mindful of the values that guide your responses—makes an enormous difference. As one leader told me, good management comes from best practices; good leadership comes from deep practice, the inner work of gaining self-knowledge. Courageous leadership is both.

> We must find a way to live in the continuing conversation, with all its conflicts and complexities, while staying in close touch with our own inner teacher.
> —Parker J. Palmer

A Wholehearted Response

When faced with a tension—whether that's a long-standing, unresolved question or someone's sudden, unexpected behavior—we all have a choice. We can react out of habit, reflex, or stress, or we can respond with calmness that allows us to hold the tension in a generative way. Either our default modes of fight, flight, freeze, or flock kick in—or we decide to choose a more constructive, wholehearted response.

A capacity to hold tension in life-giving ways comes from being fortified with language, practices, community, and a growth mindset so that creative possibilities can emerge. "Holding tension" doesn't mean ignoring it or being frozen with indecision. Instead it's a dynamic, active practice. Holding tension is the act of stretching open something within you. Think of tension as opening the heart and opening the mind, so that under tension they don't shatter: they expand.

Holding tension is an inner process of owning your emotions, even processing them for several days if needed. That "holding" can be done with people you trust. It's a process of checking in on your feelings and asking whether you're on the right track so that you can overcome insecurity and trust your own voice. It helps you move from frustration toward a vision of what ought to be. Holding tension, rather than reacting, allows you to take time to sit with feelings and thoughts that can lead to a creative response.

Notice that when you're holding a tension, there's an energy flow. Sometimes it's the energy of anger; sometimes it's surprise or excitement, curiosity, or just trying to figure things out. The first thing energy does is to open you. Then you can figure out how to use the energy to *move* to something new. Think of the positive and negative poles of a battery. Polarity generates energy to create power, to empower, to fuel something new. There's no energy in a battery until you connect the poles, close the circuit. The tension between the poles of knowing and not knowing, for example, can create an energy to learn.

It takes courage to create connections, not only between opposite conditions or between polarized people but also between head, heart, and gut. Our entire lives are based on tension, on the holding of opposites, which is part "practicing paradox."

The tension always feels difficult, sometimes destructive. But if I can collaborate with the work it is trying to do rather than resist it, the tension will not break my heart—it will make my heart larger.

—Parker J. Palmer

Holding the Tension of the Moment

Kate Sheppard had a traumatic year that included being a civilian first responder to a fatal multicar accident, divorce, and depression, on top of difficult times in her work to equip emerging and seasoned leaders with change management skills. During that year, Kate frequently referenced Parker Palmer's *A Hidden Wholeness.* His ideas for how to recognize and access inner wholeness in the midst of hard times resonated strongly. That inspired her to attend several of our retreats. What she appreciated the most was being invited to bring her whole self to the moment, without an impetus to "fix, save, or advise," and to build a trustworthy community around respectful and meaningful conversation. Those principles and practices have changed her as a leader and the way she sees her role in facilitating groups.

One day, Kate was working with an ongoing group of leaders who were responsible for departments, branches, and teams of hundreds of people. "In this particular month, our meeting was on the heels of a mass shooting and also a police shooting in our city. We were midway through our program and had a curriculum that was set out for the day."

Kate acknowledged that in the past she would have been tempted to continue on with the curriculum as planned, noting that her default leadership mode was to be the expert in the room. However, she now had a new lens on leadership, which she said is "the power of being present and with people on their journey."

So that day in San Francisco after the shootings, Kate recognized a chance to show up in a supportive and responsive way for the participants in her program. She threw out the curriculum for the morning and instead just asked people to talk about what they were thinking and feeling about the recent events she knew were on all their minds. The first hour, people talked about feeling helpless and despairing, but the second hour's talk turned toward what they could do to effect change, how to remember to be grateful for what they have, and how to be encouraging of one another and their staffs. Two hours in, Kate asked the group, *What does everyone need now?* They all agreed to return to the curriculum for the rest of the day.

The result was healing and empowering at the same time. Leaders thanked her for creating space for the conversation and for acknowledging that this was not a time for "business as usual."

Kate's story of taking time to process emotions happened to be fresh in our minds at the Center for Courage & Renewal in November 2016 and inspired us to follow her lead. It was the day after the presidential election, when so many seemed stunned by the results. We all knew people who had called in sick to avoid work that day or were distracted by angry messages exploding on Facebook or were tiptoeing around, not knowing who thought what. All nine of us were in the office that Wednesday morning and one more from his remote office was ready to phone in, but nobody was in the mood for our weekly tactical meeting. Hearts were too full for heads to fully engage.

Instead we decided to use that time to share any feelings aloud with each other and talk about the complexity of the moment. After an hour, we were able to go on with the work of our day. And the days after that. We fortified ourselves by coming together as a small community, not to fix each other or stoke the flames of negative emotions, but simply to be present to what was authentic and real for each person that day.

We dug into our inner resources for self-knowledge, we dug into our resource of community for connection, and we dug into our quote archives to find words of wisdom from our guy, Parker Palmer, which we shared outward into our virtual community: "The spiritual life is lived in a balance of paradoxes, and the humility that enables us to hear the truth of others must stand in creative tension with the faith that empowers us to speak our own."[1]

The last of the human freedoms—to choose one's attitude

in any given set of circumstances, to choose one's own way.
—Viktor Frankl

Turning to Wonder with a Broken-Open Heart

As the education director for the Santa Ynez Band of Chumash Indians, Sandoval is responsible for forty-five staff members who are working to improve lifelong educational outcomes for tribal community members. On the day we met, she was having a discussion with two early-career staff members about a project to expand their social media reach. She was consciously resisting the urge to problem-solve and instead trying to hold the tension between voicing her concerns and offering support for their creative ideas. And she was trying to stay focused, even though she was distracted by a difficult family situation she had been facing the previous day.

In a bizarre incident two years earlier, Niki's sister had been driving under the influence of nitrous oxide when she struck another vehicle. The result was a casualty, killing the driver, who was a former teacher of Niki's sister at the local high school. Niki's sister had been struggling with addiction and health issues that had gone undiagnosed, but until then she had lived a responsible life with no criminal history. Niki was heartbroken for everyone involved. The legal process had gone on for more than two years.

The day before we met, Niki's sister had been sentenced to nearly fourteen years in state prison. Niki and the victim's family were present. Niki really wanted to acknowledge them in their grief and express her sorrow in person. (She had written a letter to them months earlier, but had to keep her distance during the legal process.) On that day, Niki was afraid of igniting their anger. Still unsure, Niki walked past the family standing outside the courthouse, her head hanging down and feeling heavy.

"Then something stopped me, and I acknowledged to myself that I was afraid of doing what I wanted to do as a human." She backed up and walked over to the familiar faces and said, "Excuse me, I don't mean to interrupt, but I want to tell you how sorry I am for your loss. I couldn't walk by and not acknowledge you. I'm her sister, and I'm so sorry."

The dead woman's husband came over and embraced her in a big bear hug, saying, "Niki, I know who you are, and I know you do a lot of good in the community." He was crying, too.

That decision to speak to the family was the right thing to do, for Niki's own healing and for the other family's. She connected from a heartfelt wish to be compassionate, without expecting a reciprocal response.

"I'm glad I made that choice," Niki told me. "I think I'm a lot more willing now to make choices like that. Even if the outcome is not what I want, I wonder what can I learn from it, how can I grow."

"*When the going gets tough, turn to wonder* is a touchstone I've revisited through this tragedy," Niki said. "I've always been afraid of conflict my whole life. But now I've been able to look at fear, face it, and then try to have the courage to confront it."

Niki described how her heart "broke open" during the two years of legal proceedings and in connecting with the victim's family. The moment she took a leap of courage to express her true self was another step in that journey. "When the gentleman embraced me, it was such an authentic and true human connection that I physically felt a release of this congestion that had been building up." Niki's heart-awakening journey affected more than her personal life. It changed how Niki showed up at work.

Violence is what happens when we don't know what else to do with our own suffering, writes Parker Palmer. But courage prevented Niki's heartbreak from causing collateral damage at work. It could have been quite understandable, even forgivable, if Niki were short tempered, distant, even weepy at times—but that wasn't her style. Instead, Niki's reflective capacity and courage created the opposite result: authenticity, wholeness, and meaning.

"This whole last couple of years has just broken me open. Only three weeks ago a colleague said to me, 'Niki, I don't know what's happened with you, but this year you are different. I don't know how to say it, but you are delightful. You are very pleasant and funny. I don't know why you are different, but you just are, and I want you to know that I really like you.'"

Even though they had always had a good relationship, Niki's colleague recognized a surprising, paradoxical change. Niki tried to name it: "In one sense, I've been broken open through the darkness. One of the lessons my sister has taught us as a family is that you really have to relish every moment because in the blink of an eye your life can change. She has been living in a concrete box for the last two years when before she had lived a life of freedom. Things like birthday parties or going to work in the morning, things that we would think are mundane, they are really not; they are gifts at every opportunity. It's how you approach them that makes all the difference."

A Triad of Touchstones

In all my interviews, three touchstones stood out as the keys leaders have come to use when facing challenges: turning to wonder when the going gets rough, resisting the urgency to fix or save others, and asking open, honest questions. Setting aside judgment and remaining curious create a growth mindset. Realizing that some situations are not yours to fix results in more patience and perspective. You can at least ask yourself, *What can I learn from all this?* And when you can access a calmness to proceed, you can also access more generative questions. You can stay engaged in the challenge without giving up. Rather than either-or polarized choices, a third way can emerge.

A certain story kept coming across my awareness that seems to reinforce the value of beneficial curiosity, especially in troubled times. Do you know the legend of Perceval and the Fisher King? (There are many versions.) Perceval is a teenager who grew up hearing tales of King Arthur and the

Holy Grail. When he is finally old enough, he goes to the castle hoping to become one of the brave knights. But times had changed, and the glory days were gone. The king was injured in the groin and thus unable to procreate, and he had fallen into deep despair. Without the bright leader, the kingdom also fell into ruin. Perceval wants to ask the king what's wrong, but he doesn't want to be rude, so he goes to bed without saying a word. He wakes up and finds that the kingdom is deserted. Perceval leaves, setting out on his own quest for the grail. He comes to find out that if he had asked the question, the king could have been healed. Years later, Perceval returns and finds the old king alone on the riverbank fishing. This time Perceval asks the question, *What ails thee?* A spell is broken, and instantly the king and the kingdom are restored to health.

I learned that Perceval's name comes from the phrase "pierce the valley" and represents the concept of piercing through polarities, past the dyad of one and two, and across the threshold to three—the triad, the triangle, the structure that creates space. The triad gives us a beginning, middle, and end; dawn, noon, dusk; past, present, future; input, output, throughput; fight, flight, fortify. The triangle is seen in countless corporate logos, signifying a message of wholeness, strength, stability, and process.[2]

Perceval's story confirms both the importance of asking good questions and the consequence of the unasked question. But it also speaks of the journey each person must take to become aware of self and of others. Leadership is being able to find the way through.

A Caution About Wonder

A problem arises when we take "wonder" and "no fixing" too literally and refuse to apply the third touchstone, which is to ask open, honest questions. There's a fine line between having patience while someone explores his dilemma and not waiting too long before offering support to help him come through to the other side.

Please don't use turning to wonder as a reason to lapse into benign neglect or to ignore someone's suffering. How do you know if he's stuck? When he seems unable to access his inner resources. Beneficial curiosity is called for, and compassion. That can start with a question: *What ails thee?* This doesn't translate into "Here, let me fix things for you." It translates into "I see you are suffering. What's that about?"

Follow-up questions can unlock options for moving forward, as Mike's questions did with Bob (chapter 8), as Jill's did with the janitor, converting the typical polarity of management and labor into a positive resolution. Even Kate began with a question that shifted the energy toward healing: *How are you feeling about the violence you're seeing?* Then she asked the follow-up question, *What would you like to do next?*

10

The Courage to Choose Wisely

> I want my inner truth to be the plumb line for the choices I make about my life—about the work that I do and how I do it, about the relationships I enter into and how I conduct them.
> —Parker J. Palmer

Greg Eaton, whom we met in chapter 8, faced a difficult time as a business owner in the years following the 2008 recession. "I was constantly stretched by the reality of living through '08, '09, '10, when the economy was so tough. Wanting to keep the company healthy and profitable and also care for the workforce I care so deeply about, as so many things are shifting ... Talk about tension."

In his business organizing corporate meetings and incentive trips, Greg wanted his employees to be as productive as possible and to enjoy what they did—because when they did, it showed. "We clearly are in business to assist clients at a high level of excellence. But what do we do internally for the people here who give the best hours of their day, year after year, to this work so that they feel engaged and know that they're cared about? That's what kept me awake during those lean years."

Of course his employees knew the economy was in a rough spot, but they didn't know the extent of Greg's concern. "I was torn between not wanting, but wanting to share a little bit of that tension. And I wanted to demonstrate that I believed in them, as individuals, and that I had confidence that we would get through it."

Greg was faced with many difficult decisions affecting the bottom line, including rapidly escalating health insurance costs. Although the company covered the employee portion, Greg was aware that the big increase in premium costs meant that many employees were not purchasing additional coverage for their spouses and children. With significant price differences among plan options, he could have made a swift unilateral decision to select the least expensive plan. But Greg chose a different path that aligned with his and the company's stated values to always relate in an open, honest, direct, and caring manner.

He wanted to bring people from different departments together and have a conversation about choosing a health insurance plan, so he sent out materials for his staff to read in advance, with questions to reflect on as well. Greg explained in advance that when they all came together to talk, they would listen to each other share about how plan options might impact families or spouses. He told them, "We're not just going to dive in to which plan do we want, but we are going to spend some time looking at the whole person you bring to the room and the other whole people in the room. We're not always aware of what's going on for one another. I might make difference choices if I know more."

On the day of the meeting, people had individual time to reflect and write down their thoughts. Next, they sat together in smaller groups where they could safely share a little bit aloud and hear the questions that others were asking. "By the time the discussion moved back to the larger group, the rough edges of thought were gone, and the collective truth was more well defined," Greg said.

Greg noted how helpful it was for everyone to prepare for speaking honestly to each other. He watched as people stepped out of their own context and saw a bigger picture. He could see them realizing the ways that different health plans would affect others. As they shared their stories, they began to see that maybe another option would be better for all of them as a whole.

In the end, the decision was Greg's, but the staff supported his choice because they had heard one another's concerns and understood Greg's convictions. The process increased their personal regard and respect for each other as human beings, which is essential to building more relational trust (as we discussed in chapter 4).

Greg recognizes that people become more invested and engaged as employees when they reflect on their own choices and attitudes. By offering a reflective process to his staff that honored their wholeness and trusted their capacity for empathy and dialogue, Greg increased the chances that their own internal plumb lines would guide them, which enhanced their sense of commitment to and fulfillment in their work. But it all started with Greg's internal choice to lead with integrity.

A man or woman becomes fully human only by his or her choices. People attain worth and dignity by the multitude of decisions they make from day to day. These decisions require courage.
—Rollo May

Choosing to Risk

Leaders make countless decisions every day, many of which are invisible to others in their organization. They get credit (or criticism) for prominent decisions, whether those lead to success or failure. Yet the subtle decisions that appreciate over time are those that leave their true mark.

What is the best decision you ever made? The worst? What is the best decision you *never* made? Many leaders say that the best decisions are often the ones that involved risk without guarantee of reward—ones that took courage.

Leadership is not about making *bold* decisions but about making life-affirming, thoughtful, well-intentioned choices—and sometimes delaying decisions, too, to allow for better solutions to emerge (in other words, allowing doubt to make space for other options to appear).

Many decisions by necessity carry more weight, even risk, and leaders are trained and compensated for being able to take the right risks at the right time. But wise decisions are not always big, visible pronouncements. Some decisions are internal—such as how Greg Eaton chooses to care for his staff because of his own values as a leader.

It's risky to try new ways of being in conversation. It's risky to engage participation that could change your own views. It's risky to be your whole self. As Dawna Markova writes, "I choose to risk my significance," choosing to live less afraid.[1]

Is there another way to think of risk management? Of course you have to weigh options to ensure that you have good information about the facts, clarity about the possible pros and cons, and the right inputs from others who know more than you do. "Quick and bold" decisions may be more about preserving the status quo for safety's sake. But risk-taking is more artful when it is based in an open-minded approach, trusting that another, more unusual choice might be possible once you go inward to reflect and to align with the whole.

I wonder if you can get still enough—not quiet enough—still enough to hear rumbling up from your unique and essential idiom, the sound of the genuine in you.
—Howard Thurman

The Courage to Renew and Reinvent

In 2011, Stephen Lewis became president of the Forum for Theological Exploration (FTE) in Atlanta, Georgia. Since its founding in 1954, FTE has been in the business of discernment, helping young leaders explore their passion, purpose, and call by exploring such questions as *Who am I? What are my gifts? And how am being called to live into those gifts in the world?*

FTE discovered that the same discernment practices to gain "vocational clarity" for individuals were instructive for an organization as a whole. In the aftermath of the 2008–2009 recession, FTE faced serious questions about its identity and purpose. There had been a turnover of three presidents in eight years, and FTE needed to discern its next faithful steps and strategic direction in the face of changing times.

Stephen was inspired to frame FTE's strategic planning process around Parker Palmer's Habits of the Heart: (1) recognizing that we're all in this together; (2) appreciating the value of otherness; (3) holding tensions in life-giving ways; (4) cultivating a sense of personal voice and agency; and (5) having the capacity to create community.

FTE decided to undertake eight listening tours with two hundred people over the course of eighteen months. In retreat formats conducted with their hybrid version of the touchstones, which they call Conversation Covenants, FTE posed such questions as *What kind of leaders do we need now? What attributes would such leaders have? What are the leadership challenges you're facing in your own context?*

Each Habit of the Heart came into play during that time.

1. **Recognizing that we're all in this together** affirms that an organization is more than the leader in the corner office, more than the staff, more even than the clients and stakeholders. It affirms the power of wholeness. FTE knew that face-to-face conversations would be the most generative way to glean collective wisdom. More than simply gaining

others' opinions, the process created a sense of collective buy-in.

2. **Appreciating the value of otherness** allows an organization to leverage differences in a healthy, not manipulative, way. A team can exist and thrive only when its members value each other's perspectives. But the idea was larger than that for FTE. As a sixty-year-old organization, FTE had primarily worked with constituents in the Protestant mainline. Recognizing that the Christian community of faith is much broader than that prompted FTE to prioritize building relationships with people, partners, collaborators, and allies of different theological perspectives. "We recognized this whole notion that these others bring particular gifts to our work and to our conversation that are missing," said Stephen.

3. **Holding tensions in life-giving ways** affirms the practice and power of paradox. FTE's tension is in recognizing that despite an overall decline of Christianity in North America, it is growing within communities of color and immigrant communities of color. Another

tension is the declining enrollment across the board in higher education, particularly within theological institutions—yet there is fast-growing enrollment among communities of color. The paradox of decline and growth revealed an opportunity for FTE to refocus its efforts with a greater commitment to diversity and inclusion of communities of color, whereas their ministry focus in the first sixty years had primarily served white Mainline Christian communities.

A third layer of tension is that young adults want to make a difference in the world; the tension lies in trying to understand how faith informs the ways in which they can live a faithful life of service when they don't necessarily see a community of faith, or Christian communities, as the primary place in which they can attend to their deepest passion or sense of call in the world.

"The question then is," said Stephen, "how do we develop strategies that recognize that some people will want to be and serve as leaders within a traditional church context. Other people will want to serve in leadership for the church in very innovative and new emerging ways. Still there'll be others who want to be ministry leaders in other organizational forms."

Successful strategies can emerge when leaders understand the complex landscape in which they operate and can hold multiple tensions, not in an antagonistic way but in a both-and relationship. As the three examples in the previous paragraphs reveal, there isn't just one set of tensions, but many—which is true of the complex world in which we live and work today. Paradox often looks more like a daisy of many petals than a two-pronged pair of opposites.

4. **A sense of personal voice and agency** affirms that everyone's voice needs to be heard and that all of us can make a difference. Gaining clarity about your vocation is a process of listening for and answering where the world is calling you to apply your unique gifts, talents, and graces. Organizations must ask, *What is our unique niche? What is our value proposition? What is it that we as an*

organization uniquely offer to our field? What is it that we offer to the bigger world? What is it that we offer to our constituency that they may not get anywhere else in particular?

Organizations can have a vocation—a sense of voice and agency. So at FTE they ask the question this way: *What aspect of the future will never come to fruition if we do not answer our call as an organization or take our next most faithful steps toward that call?*

Stephen noted, "This habit helps us remember that FTE's voice is one of many in the ecology of voices and institutions that are trying to find their own unique niche in service to creating the world anew." Part of that is about vision and mission, but it's also about strategic and scenario planning. FTE asked, *What is our unique sense of voice and agency when the economy is strong and people have good feelings about religion and communities of faith and leaders of faith in particular?* FTE's voice and agency would need to look vastly different when the economy is not strong and there's waning interest within communities of faith. By considering different scenarios, FTE could think strategically about how best to be agile and exercise its agency and voice in different scenarios of possible futures.

5. **A capacity to create community** affirms the importance of an interdependent web of relationships in fostering the other Habits of the Heart. That's why FTE spent more than a year listening to stakeholders and potential partners who knew or were aware of FTE and could help the organization become more self-aware and grow into greater clarity about its mission and work. Stakeholders serve as a mirror and reflect what those inside an organization cannot always see. FTE had the courage to risk being vulnerable and to listen not only for its strengths but also for where it needed to grow and improve. It was willing to do so because FTE leaders trusted their partners. As Howard Thurman once said, and as Stephen and the FTE team knew, "I can run the risk of radical exposure and know that the eye that beholds my vulnerability will not step on me."[2]

What came out of FTE's listening process was greater clarity about its strategic direction. Stephen summed up what people said: "If FTE doesn't do anything else, I hope it will continue to build a platform and its reputation to convene meaningful conversations about the next generation of leaders shaping the future of the church and academy." This was an important insight for FTE because there is a distinction between convening meaningful conversation and hosting conferences or events. That clarity informed the organization's changing its name (but not its acronym) from the Fund for Theological Education to the Forum for Theological Exploration.

"With a little creativity and a little courage," said Stephen, "people can pivot and advance their organizations' work in meaningful ways that help create a more hopeful future."

Trusting the Process

How often do you choose out of fear or choose out of trust? Wise choices come from clarity of thought and a connection to what you can trust deep inside. Your wise inner leader has integrated all your skills, talents, experience, competencies, and capacities, as well as the facts you have gathered, and is accessible to guide your actions and choices.

Examining good data helps us gain much-needed clarity and alignment. And even then, all the data in the world can't always guarantee the results needed. Good leadership is not about *controlling* outcomes but about responding to the current knowns and trusting yourself and your team despite the unknowns.

Having access to your inner resources and the support of a committed group of people fortifies you to take risks to choose wisely and to know that, no matter what happens next, you're still in it together, capable of meeting whatever comes.

A RUBRIC FOR CHOOSING WITH INTEGRITY

An emphasis on the inner life and interpersonal dynamics can inform decision making beyond the usual analytical tools. You can look past externals and see to another way of approaching and thinking about this important part of your role. Try these reflective practices.

First, look within to your true self. Seek self-awareness. Be honest with your true self. What is it you fear? Why are you saying no—because of expediency and efficiency, or because it is the right answer? How are your shadows interfering with clarity? Where are the unnamed elephants in the room? Are you one of them? Because there is often more than one, as one leader quipped, "The floor's not going to support the weight of all those elephants much longer."

Look for trust. What effect would a decision have on the trust level in your organization? Does it reflect shared values and priorities? Or does it violate them? How are regard, respect, competence, and integrity at play in your decision? If one or more are not present, which is missing, and how can you address that lack in this moment?

Look for community. What would it take for you to risk being vulnerable? To say "I don't know" or "I need your help"? What could it look like to weigh other opinions, to gain perspective from a number of other angles, even if you don't agree with them? How might you look for abundance in your community, an abundance that can be called on to enrich your perspective? Seek situational awareness, taking into account other people and their perspectives. When purpose is clear and people trust in each other, it's possible to call on them to help find solutions and to identify those individuals who are willing to put in the energy toward making the proposed solution happen. If people don't step up to participate, could it be that the issue isn't as urgent as you may have thought? What else might their reluctance tell you?

Look for paradox. Can two seemingly incompatible ideas or factors both be true? How might you hold them in a both-and way and see how that changes your perspective? How might you look for a way to make a win-win possible? Where can both-and come into play instead of either-or?

Notice what default corner have you gone to—fight, flight, freeze, or flock. What is keeping your true self from being fully present with whatever decision you face? Do you feel defensive? Do you want to avoid it? Are you stuck in indecision? Are you being belligerent? Do you recognize any of these stress reactions as places you've gone before when faced with difficult challenges? How can you reframe where you are and transform being stuck in a corner? Which of these other practices might fortify you so that you can move forward?

Where are you on the Möbius strip? Are you stuck or in motion or sliding way off the edge? How might you seek introspection to gain an internal perspective and strength? Are you taking considered action because you've collected your thoughts, your data, and your crew of competent colleagues or community? What if trust is the glue that binds the Möbius strip: what and whom can you trust as you consider this decision? If you're hoping for creative courage—healthy risk-taking and innovation—how have you held yourself accountable as a leader to put the conditions in place for trust and courage to arise?

Each time you pause to engage in these reflective practices, you are honing your art of discernment. That improves the likelihood of making decisions with less fear and regret, with more courage and trust. Choosing wisely is a way of finding "integrity and the courage to act on it."

11

The Courage to Connect and Trust in Each Other

What I want is the impossible. I want as much diversity in things, in people, in places, in ideas as possible. But I want unity among things and people and places and ideas. I want that unity without anything losing its uniqueness.
—Emil Antonucci, illustrator and publisher

If you were to sit down in the campus dining hall at Garrett-Evangelical Theological Seminary, you would find yourself talking to students with a wide range of cultural, language, and theological backgrounds. When Lallene Rector became the new president in 2014, she wanted the school to live even further into its promise to be a place of welcome, inclusion, and diversity. She announced an institutional priority to focus for years to come on matters of race, antiviolence, white normativity and privilege, and competence in cultural diversity, so that these would become a lens through which they did all their work. One of her first matters of attention was one of focusing on creating welcome to LGBTQ persons.

Lallene's vision goes beyond having a safe and diverse campus culture. She aims to equip leaders and graduates so that they can promote understanding, dialogue, and justice in their communities. Even more important, she hopes that in the near future, more denominations will ordain ministers regardless of their sexual orientation. Those hopes and her big vision had to start with new policies at the level where Lallene holds influence as president of the seminary.

"While we had some statements from 1997 about nondiscrimination in grading policy, they were old statements and not strong enough. We could do a lot better."

Lallene also knew that new policy had to start at the personal level. So she decided to hold a dialogue process to address LGBTQ welcome and inclusivity. It would unfold in four twenty-five-person circle sessions, each with a cross-section of students, faculty, trustees, and staff. The touchstones created firm boundaries for how people would interact: *Extend and presume welcome. Set aside judgment and try compassionate inquiry instead. Avoid fixing, saving, or advising others. Speak your truth and honor others' truths. Leave room for silence...*

The dialogue sessions began with open, honest questions to guide the participants in examining their own experiences: *Turn to two people next to you and talk about a time in your life when you felt different. What did that feel like?*

Out of one hundred people, only one man (a white man) answered that he could "never" remember feeling different.

Then people talked about issues that mattered to them personally. Topics ranged from mentoring United Methodist students pursuing ordination to gender-neutral bathrooms to reexamining curriculum, and more.

"The point was not to get people to agree about the morality or rightness of how LGBTQ persons live. At the very least, we have an obligation to be welcoming and inclusive of all persons. And we need to be on record with that. I also wanted the community to go through a process to speak to this concern in safe ways, ways to let people who had different opinions speak and be heard. I knew we couldn't come to an institutional statement without a process."

"With a topic as volatile and provocative as this, with such strong feelings, it had the potential to blow up. I was determined we should do something *respectfully,* but also that we should absolutely *do something.*"

As a result of the dialogue sessions, a set of formal recommendations were presented to—and affirmed by—the board of trustees. That formal approval laid the groundwork for the next actions the school would take. Convening those dialogue sessions was not the only thing

Lallene needed to do, but they were a beginning. It was important to start by recalling a personal experience around difference to create a sense of empathy and understanding, and also to create buy-in for change initiatives.

> An institution that truly embraces Diversity as a Value commits to not only moving the furniture, but also remodeling the entire structure if necessary.
> —Sherry K. Watt, professor and facilitator

Designing Spaces to Connect Community

One of the first things Sigrid Wright did when she became CEO of the Community Environmental Council was to change the furniture and knock down walls. "It's ironic that we work hard for the environment from inside an office eight to twelve hours a day. What's worse, our space was designed like a rabbit warren with dark corridors, poor air flow, and a sense of separation."

One room they call the West Wing got a lot of natural sunlight, but a solid wall separated it from the entire east side, and it had become a place to stash people and things out of sight. So Sigrid knocked down one wall and put a hole in another, installed big French doors so that light can extend to the rest of the office, added a couple of "living walls" of plants, and created a high-visibility bike parking section to emphasize the organization's commitment to alternative transportation. "The remodel improved everyone's state of mind," Sigrid said. "The West Wing is now an integrated, visible, flexible work space with bright colored movable furniture. This has been game changing for our associates, interns, and partners, who now want to be in the office more. They're more visible when they're here, and are collaborating more because they have a place in which to creatively gather."

The remodel also helped Sigrid shift the way she holds staff meetings, moving out of the conference room with its long rectangular table. "In the conference room, whoever is leading the meeting is forced to sit at the head of the table because it's the only spot where you can make eye contact with everyone. That's fine for many things, but I wanted to bring a different tone to staff meetings." The new flexible West Wing has become the meeting room where they sit in a more casual circle; it's not unusual for one staffer's new baby to be on a blanket on the floor in the center.

The next change was more strategic in terms of inviting and welcoming a sense of shared leadership in the office. Sigrid started a process where staff rotate leading the bimonthly meetings. "Staff each have different needs and different definitions of leadership. The ones who want more emotional connection might choose to open with an icebreaker to ask everyone how they are feeling. Others choose to open with a warm-up exercise on big-picture visioning. In one meeting, a staff member led us through an exercise to articulate our personal values.

"Those changes have been really helpful, because (a) it creates space for others to step into their own leadership however they define that, and (b) it's one place staff can start to be more self-aware about what *they* need to be healthy, happy, and productive in their jobs and make it happen for themselves, rather than reflect it back to me about what's missing from the staff meeting. I say, 'Bring it in yourself!'"

Another significant change Sigrid made was to clear one afternoon each week for anyone who wants to book time with her. It has helped her personally and is good for her team. "The daily disruption factor is a challenge of managers across the universe. I was finding that I was responding to problems or issues as if they were tennis balls: *whack, whack.* This wasn't giving anyone a chance to really learn or grow. My door is still open all week, but if the discussion can wait till Tuesday afternoon, then it gives me a chance to put away other work and move into a place of deeper listening." All this invokes the second touchstone: *Be present as fully as possible.* Sigrid also said, "I try to ask open, honest questions to help them figure out what to do, rather than me simply giving them quick solutions."

Peter Block writes that transformation occurs when leaders focus on the structure of how people gather. Leadership is "convening," he says, and happens when leaders can shift the context within which people gather, when they can name the debate through powerful questions, and when they listen rather than advocate, defend, or provide answers. The physical design of the spaces in which we work makes a big difference. "The design process itself needs to be an example of the future we are intending to create," Block says.[1]

Sigrid did just that when she designed her meeting room with interaction in mind. Most meeting rooms are designed for control, negotiation, and persuasion. But we can choose to rearrange the furniture to facilitate how we interact in those spaces. Living into those values day after day is the real test of integrity. You can see a glimpse of that in Sigrid's intention and presence when she meets with her staff in groups and individually.

Physical space must be met with open minds and open hearts, and a willingness to be changed. How often have you been welcomed into a new job but not felt really welcome to bring something new? The phrase "That's not how things are done here" doesn't make room for learning and growth. True welcome also means welcoming different routines and traditions, as well as welcoming how people express themselves through their work. It takes courage and good questions—at the very least—to explore what new things might be possible to cocreate going forward.

In diversity there is beauty and there is strength. We all should know that diversity makes for a rich tapestry, and we must understand that all the threads of that tapestry are equal in value no matter their color.

—Maya Angelou

Welcoming All Sorts of Diversity

At work and at home, what are the ways you have experienced hospitality and welcome—or the absence of welcome? When have you been in a space where people felt seen, heard, valued, and safe?

Kate Sheppard described what welcome feels like, especially for an introvert like herself who often feels intimidated in a crowd of people she doesn't know. At her first retreat sitting in a large circle of strangers, she reached down into her bag to get out a pen. At that moment, the lead facilitator, Marcy Jackson, tried to squeeze by her chair, and Kate blurted out, "Oh, my gosh, I'm so sorry," apologizing for blocking Marcy's passage. A typical interaction in that moment would have been for Marcy to reply, "No problem." Instead Marcy saw it as an opportunity to recognize Kate; she put her hand on Kate's shoulder, saying, "Oh Kate, I'm so glad you're here. Thank you for coming."

How Marcy responded affected Kate deeply. "To me that embodied the spirit of welcoming others into a safe space and put me at ease for the rest of the retreat."

Welcome and inclusion can be as simple as making sure there are enough chairs at the table for all meeting participants. Welcome is making eye contact and saying hello to your coworkers or anyone who walks into your space. Or ensuring that people can talk while sitting side by side rather than separated by a large, power-laden desk during a difficult conversation. If you work in a global organization, inclusion can mean being aware of the time zones, not always scheduling meetings in the wee hours for those farthest away. Food allergies, differences in religious holidays, or differences in lifestyle (for example, being parents or being single)—all are opportunities to examine equity and inclusion. When you start to think about all the ways people are different and about which policies tend to favor one over another, you can become overwhelmed—or you can see a rich source of topics for curiosity-filled conversation.

Describing this variety of efforts to offer welcome and inclusion is not meant to dismiss or deny the more painful and complex realities of today's world—realities such as structural racism and oppression of marginalized people that are deeply rooted in society.

Professor and Courage & Renewal facilitator Sherry K. Watt told me, "We must acknowledge the ugly and the darkness as much as the light and not move too quickly past it. If more people could find a way to focus on the system and not on the people they think they're fighting, I think we could find ways to dismantle the system that is binding us all."

In her book *Designing Transformative Multicultural Initiatives*, Watt introduces the metaphor of "moving the furniture" as a way to name the structural barriers that must be dismantled. "Making this shift requires a focus on developing the skills to engage in difficult dialogue in productive and principled ways," she writes. Such difficult dialogue must occur within authentic relationships that honor one another's individual identities, values, and beliefs.[2]

"We have to recognize how heavy the furniture is [of structural racism in the United States, for example]. It has nails that go deep into the foundation," Watt told me. "You need a lot of people to rock and rock to move it just a little bit. We recognize there is furniture and it needs moving—and we need to sit with how heavy the furniture is before we talk about strategies for moving it."

She writes, "The aim is to actively and critically interrogate the historical and contemporary roots of traditions and practices (head), to explore self in relation to context of the point of conflict in authentic and self-awakening ways (heart), and then balance reflection of the former with taking collectively thoughtful and socially just action (hands) to change the environment."[3]

Like the poets, scientists tell us that biodiversity is the planet's saving grace, and that it is in the places where there is the most diversity—they call it the "growing edge"—that living things flourish. Yet flourishing has to do with sustaining the struggle, staying in the discomfort, long enough for growth to occur. There isn't a quick fix for overcoming generations of cultural conditioning and systemic oppression. It is a process without certain outcomes. And because it's a process that must engage people—their heads, hands, and hearts—it takes courage and trust.

> Here is your life. You might never have been, but you are because the party wouldn't have been complete without you.
> —Frederick Buechner

Welcoming the Soul Without an Agenda

Touchstones are one example of guidelines for creating trustworthy and disciplined space in which to hold meaningful conversations. Over the years, our touchstones have been used with skilled facilitation to hold conversations around race, class, sexual orientation, and other potentially divisive matters. But there is a paradox here, because "to invite the soul to show up in order to solve a social problem is to scare it away as surely as when we set out to fix another person." The soul can be approached for no other reason than to honor it without trying to direct or demand certain outcomes.[4]

In his book *A Hidden Wholeness,* Parker Palmer describes being approached by the leaders of a community whose schools were being torn by racial and ethnic tensions. They wanted his help in creating Circles of Trust to alleviate this crisis. As much as he cared about their plight, Parker had to tell them he could not help—at least, not under those circumstances—because their request reflected a misconception of what makes a circle trustworthy to the soul.

> You cannot gather people and say, in effect, "In this circle, we invite your soul to speak so we can resolve our racial tensions." The moment you do so, an impossible distortion sets in: I am in the circle because I have a "white soul," he is here because he has an "African

American soul," and she is here because she has a "Hispanic soul." But the soul has no race or ethnicity: it is the core of our shared humanity as well as our individual uniqueness. The moment we try to trap it in sociological categories, hoping to get leverage on some problem, it will run away as fast as it can because we have distorted its nature.[5]

This raises the question of whether it's possible to create truly safe space when talking about emotionally charged issues. It's not meant to dismiss that social categories do exist (race, class, ethnicity, and so on), which makes holding the many tensions at any one time exceedingly complex. Meaningful conversations about things that matter require trust.

Inclusion asks, "Has everyone's ideas been heard?" Justice responds, "Whose ideas won't be taken as seriously because they aren't in the majority?"

—Dafina-Lazarus Stewart, PhD

Safe Space or Brave Space?

It takes courage to let oneself be exposed to differences that are threatening for whatever reason. It takes courage to sit in a room with people you don't know, when you can't anticipate how others will react to your words. But dialogue ground rules such as the touchstones define the agreed parameters in which people can take the risk to speak about how they think and feel. In such a circle, people respond to the invitation to be empathetic to others: "Oh, is that what you're experiencing? I had no idea."

Lallene acknowledges that there is no such thing as entirely safe space: "We can't be protected from our anxiety. But we can create a place of respect where nobody is coerced to speak. Having a well-facilitated experience around speaking up can encourage people to continue to try to do that or engage further conversations elsewhere in their lives."

The term *safe space* has itself become a hot-button phrase in recent years, especially on college campuses and social justice settings where it is sometimes invoked as a way to avoid conflict rather than to engage differences with respect. Brian Arao and Kristi Clemens investigated this phenomenon and discovered that their students were conflating safety with comfort.[6] When dialogue moved from polite to provocative, students were invoking "safe space" for protection—but not so much as protection of free speech as protection against anxiety. Feeling defensive, students slipped into a default mode where they discounted, deflected, or retreated from a challenge. The authors wonder whether this kind of response occurred because students were not adequately and honestly prepared to be challenged in this way. "Were we in fact hindering our own efforts by relying on the traditional language of safe space?" they ask. Rather than claiming to remove risk from the equation, Arao and Clemens opt for different language, emphasizing the importance of bravery to help students understand and rise to meet the challenges of genuine dialogue.[7]

It takes courage to step into unconventional conversations that ask us to examine our hearts, our actions, our assumptions, and the implicit biases that occupy our blind spots. Such conversations can bring up a variety of negative emotions, ranging from fear and sorrow to guilt and anger. They can trigger memories of feeling violated, or realizations of being the one perpetrating violence. They become uncomfortable very quickly, and it's hard to stay in discomfort and to stay open to the conversation.

But when we actually articulate something—either writing it on paper in a journal or, more powerfully, sharing with another person, talking to another person—that's when our experience becomes more real for us. That's why it's important to create conditions that are more hospitable than the environments we usually find ourselves in.

The courage to connect depends on welcoming and valuing "otherness." Authentic leadership is showing people that you value their unique contributions and welcome diversity—in visible and invisible forms we may not always be able to measure by externals. And if you expect people to show up, to be self-aware and authentic, you as the leader have to model the behavior you are demanding.

In the company of strangers, we can learn that we are all in this together despite our many differences; that some of our differences are enriching and those that are vexing are negotiable; that it is possible to do business amicably with one another even in the face of conflicting interests.
—Parker J. Palmer

Setting the Table for Genuine Welcome

Our touchstones have made their way into a variety of other applications beyond our programs, sometimes customized to suit the needs of specific audiences and aims. The Welcome Table is one such process originally developed by Susan Glisson and her team at the William Winter Institute for Racial

Reconciliation at the University of Mississippi[8] and is a central part of her work with Sustainable Equity, the consulting firm she developed with her life partner, Charles Tucker. They work with major corporations, police departments, and public institutions to foster dialogues in racial reconciliation. Charles says their goal is to "work ourselves out of a job."

When communities and organizations invite Susan and her colleagues to bring the Welcome Table process, the invitation comes with a readiness to talk about racial issues but also pessimism. Sometimes it's possible to jump into the topic head first, often with the facilitator asking as the first question, *When did you first notice race as an elephant in the room?* At other times, it's better to encourage people to talk about their own lives, and one way to do that is with creative exercises that get people out of their heads and into their hearts.

To help people develop more ability to check in with their own feelings, the Welcome Table facilitators use an exercise called Where I'm From, inspired by the poet George Ella Lyons.[9] (Many other dialogue-based programs employ this beautiful poetry exercise, too.) Participants are invited to answer the question "Where are you from?" by recalling specific memories of their origins: items found around the home, yard, or the neighborhood where they grew up (for example, bobby pins, Grandma's front stoop, broken rakes, the corner store); names of people from the past, or family sayings; or other things, such as the names of foods or dishes or music.

Susan's own poem includes this stanza:

> I'm from Mama's dressing and
> sweet potato casserole, from
> her never taking a sick day and
> never getting to go to college
> so making sure I did.

Charles starts his poem this way:
> I am from flat brown earth
> From fields that stretched into the
> horizon with no end in sight.
> I am from crepe myrtle and black
> walnut trees, pecan groves, and
> old

King Cotton—no longer king anymore.

"Every time we tell people 'You're going to write a poem,' they freak out," Susan told me. "They're scared, like, oh my God I'm not a poet, what are you talking about, please don't, and please don't make me read it out loud.

"The prompts help people tap into long-lost thought about their families and how they grew up. They start to jostle with each other about who's going to read their poem first. I've never heard a poem that wasn't beautiful."

People have told Susan that they've framed their poem and given it to their families, or that they've kept writing the poem in a different way every day. This clearly is more than a poetry exercise. Fundamentally, the reflecting and the writing and reading of the poem—and working through it together with others—help people see that it's okay to be who they are and okay to be intimidated or uncomfortable but to go ahead anyway. After that, facilitators can introduce topics that might make participants uncomfortable, and "they've gotten a little bit of practice in about how to keep staying at the table even when [they're] uncomfortable."

A surprising aspect of creating trust among people, Susan explained, is to introduce the idea of self-care during the Welcome Table process. It's important for people to be able to trust that others are psychologically and emotionally able to be present. Stress increases our tendency to default to our implicit biases. When stress turns toxic, it's hard to predict how people will react, and that suspends trust.

Susan observed, "On some level it feels like we're sharing things that are commonsensical. But we're so distracted in a media-driven, twenty-four-hour news cycle culture, we do not stop and think. We move on to the next urgent thing. I think we're all overwhelmed and exhausted. We have got to take the time to pause and reflect and connect and breathe together. Listen to our inner teacher."

People usually resist Susan's call for self-care, saying that it sounds like a luxury and there's no time for luxuries. But when they do come into the process, those same people have come out and said, "This is not a luxury; this is a necessity." Susan named a specific urgency as an example: "Police officers go from one horrific crime scene to a traffic stop with no decompression in between. They're all walking around traumatized. We're expecting them to then have the self-discipline not to react out of old patterns. It's ridiculous."

It's also important to note that speaking about your experience and living in alignment with who you are are forms of self-care. That is care of *true self.*

Susan has facilitated remarkable changes over the years in places hurting from deep divides. I asked her, "What's one thing people could do to start building a bridge across lines of difference? What would be the first step?"

She replied, "I really wish that people would realize they can just start right where they are. They can start in their family. They can start with their friends. It doesn't require you to go to Washington, DC, or do anything complicated. Just start reaching out to people and inviting the conversation. Do it in a way that's respectful and not blaming and shaming. That might take some practice, but I think people will respond to that."

Where do you stand on complex issues like race? What would it take for you to initiate a conversation about differences—or some form of "elephant in the room" in your own workplace?

12

The Courage to Stay or to Leave

When is it that I know I have to
go someplace else?
When I have to grow—
Or die.

—Diana Chapman Walsh, "Potbound"

Dave Boyer started his engineering career at ITW, a large manufacturing company headquartered in Chicago. As a product designer on the fast track, Dave was in the leadership development program and rose quickly to account management and then to manufacturing manager within a few years. Although he was doing well financially, the stress of the job was taking its toll on his health. He told me, "Physically I wasn't doing that well. I had ulcerative colitis at the time because I was carrying the stress in my abdomen."

Then Dave got a call recruiting him to join a much smaller business in Madison, Wisconsin, a plastics packaging company. As Dave recalls it was only an $8 million company of fifty people, but he was intrigued. Dave said people told him, "Don't do it. Why would you leave this? You're successful; you're on the fast track." Dave took the new job anyway.

When I asked him why, he said, "It took a lot of courage to leave, to take the next position, but it felt like the right thing. It felt like something that would be a better fit for me. Later on I realized that I was not really cut out for the high-stakes world of being in a big corporate business. I now realize that was true then and it's probably true now, even though I was doing very well in it."

After eight years, Dave rose to CEO at the plastics packaging company. He was forty-five years old, with stock in the company, and the company was thriving. As time went by, Dave decided he wanted to own a company, primarily so that he could lead it in the way he thought was right. "I wanted to lead it in a way that I had been studying about—from an environmental sustainability standpoint, an involvement with employees standpoint, and a community involvement standpoint." He wanted to run his own company using the best in management and leadership thinking.

Dave went to the owner to give him the news. "After fifteen years, I knew he was counting on me to hang around until family members or others could come in, but I told him I had decided to leave. As I said, the company was doing well; I was doing well. There was no issue that needed to be resolved other than the fact that I wanted to do this other thing. I was aware that eventually family members would come into the business, so I left."

Making this move to own his own business entailed significant financial risk. "I basically put my entire financial life in that company, in that I had unlimited guarantees to the bank for the loans needed to buy the business. If we had failed during the two recessions that we survived, I'd have lost everything. A hundred percent, everything. Yet it seemed like the right thing to do. It turned out to be one of the most fulfilling and one of the more important things that we've done."

Dave recognizes what it took to make these leaps into the unknown. "It sure took a lot of courage to try to figure out what's in your heart, what's the right thing, where is this going, what do you want to do, where do you want to be, and then make two significant moves. I look back now after that career, and I say, 'My gosh. Either one of those could have turned out to be terrible decisions.' You just don't know until years later."

Dave's choice to leave a lucrative position not once but twice was an act of courage and an act of care for his true self. By paying attention to what truly aligned with his identity and integrity, he aligned his soul and his role. And his body seemed to appreciate the difference. After leaving his first job, his ulcerative colitis resolved. He still sees a doctor about it, but has not had any recurrence for thirty years. Dave credits good doctor care plus self-awareness and meditation. "Those were big factors at that point, to be self-aware about what is stressful to you, where your stress goes, how to manage it, how to handle it, how to know what it comes from."

Dave eventually married his business partner, Joan Philip. Together they created a company based on their values around sustainability. MCD, Inc. became known as a leadership company. It employs sixty people and specializes in products for direct mail marketing, packaging, publishing, and credit and gift cards. One of the goals Dave and Joan had was to build a culture where risk-taking is seen as an opportunity to learn. When they were ready to retire, Dave and Joan chose to sell the company to the employees by way of an employee stock ownership plan. "Selling the company to the employees was the ultimate way of fulfilling what we had been trying to create—meaning it's putting the company fully in the hands of the employees of the company."

It's worth noting that Dave's business passion does not come from a love of plastics but from his commitment to sustainability and stewardship. He told me this quick story:

"I was a frequent guest lecturer on sustainability for a local guy at the university. Almost every class I'd get the same question: 'Well, if you're so involved with sustainability, how can you possibly work for a plastics packaging firm?' I said, 'Well, I'll tell you what, if I don't work, there somebody else will, and guess how much they'll care about the environment?' I would then go on to actually encourage them to work for the dirtiest, most unsustainable company they can and cause change. We're not going to get change if all of the people who care about the environment only work for already environmentally clean organizations. The leadership in other organizations is just going to continue to do the same thing. I hope I was able to affect some of those students with that perspective."

In sharing his perspective, Dave is becoming a wise elder like the many people who lit his own path as a curious problem solver. Dave was inspired by W. Edwards Deming in terms of quality management, and then by Peter Senge in his book *The Fifth Discipline* and by books since then on systems thinking, and by Karl-Henrik Robèrt's model for sustainability and creating change. What Dave wants those young leaders to know is what he learned from Parker Palmer, that when you're looking for answers, you go inside first and second and third to inform what you do.

"Leadership comes from some place deep inside of you. All those things I learned are about not letting process and organization affect our humanity and affect our dreams.

"Don't become slaves of the organizations that you build. Processes can run awry. Don't get trapped by them. Instead, understand how the world works, what is sustainable on this earth. Understand that, teach it to other people, and always try to refer to your humanity and your dreams and your heart to find out where you are and where to go next."

Our lives begin to end the day we become silent about things that matter.
—Martin Luther King Jr.

The Courage to Leave and Still Love

"I've often felt like I have a compulsive leaving disorder," said Estrus Tucker. "That has been a big part of my professional journey. However, a closer examination of this clever play on words reveals my soul's singular struggle to be more than an occasional feel-good stand-in or bench player who gets in the game only when the outcome is certain. It takes courage and clarity to love, to leave, and still love."

That love is about staying committed to a vision and mission in life. "My hope is to be a support, a voice, and a catalyst for welcoming, embracing, and engaging a diversity of people to advance the Beloved Community that Dr. Martin Luther King Jr. dreamed of, worked toward, and died for, in Fort Worth, Texas, and the world."

Estrus has stepped down from a lot of roles where he had high hopes as the first African American man in an elevated position of organizational leadership. That's a hard place to be over time without more tangible, visible progress around inclusion of a diversity of working-class, marginalized people—the people he seeks to serve and reach. The challenge is to not become cynical and to stay faithful to your larger vision.

"When I'm in places of marginalization, where there is a disparity of services and a disparity in outcomes, I feel a sense of identity. I grew up and still live in that traditional working-class African American community. That's why affordability and access are huge lenses of leadership for me."

"What I can do most as a leader when I'm in a position of power is not forget where I'm from, not forget the perspective of people who are working and struggling, living and leading in small but significant ways. I speak truth to power because I'm often in places where if I don't, there won't be a voice."

Estrus has often felt obligated to stay in leadership positions and expand the space so that there are more opportunities for people of color. "And yet in doing so, I sacrificed my soul at times, compromising how I wanted to be in the world."

At more than one point in his career, Estrus felt like the token spokesperson when issues of inclusion and diversity became thorny. "To be the institutional champion in a community context became a tension I could not bear. What tore me was losing confidence in an institution's integrity and sincerity around issues of diversity, which were not always just about race and class. My words around diversity were quoted out of context, in ways that sometimes even justified a lack of diversity."

Feeling disillusioned, he struggled with the gap between what he was experiencing and his highest aspirations. But it was tricky to discern if he was compromising or complaining to himself.

When he felt he had to leave a position, was he doing so for the right reasons?

"If I complain too much within myself around this tension of my identity and integrity, it can feel like whining," Estrus said. "More than once I had a mentor tell me to get a grip. He'd say you can't always live out loud your highest values. This is the work. This is leadership. It's going to be hard. You have to work within the system to change it. This is life."

There's an element of truth to that, Estrus admitted, adding that it takes time to find a place to stand. "But I got to the point of realizing it was not about sucking it up and being stronger. It was clarity about how I want to contribute and lead and live in organizations."

When he discerned that the compromises were not life sustaining, Estrus acted. "It took unpopular decisions, sacrifice, and a lot of courage to let go of good things in service of a truer alignment with who I am and how I want to be in the world."

There is always a set of tensions in your role as a leader: How much of the reward is financial, or takes other forms? How does what you are receiving balance with your discernment of who you are and how you want to be in the world?

Estrus finally struck the right balance in his career by becoming an independent consultant and facilitator. His passion is to work with groups around community renewal, transformation, healing, and reconciliation. He brings his leadership to many organizations and boards, including the Center's. And he's made a difference promoting human dignity and nonviolent engagement in places like Mississippi, Texas, Northern Ireland, and South Africa.

The work he does now aligns with his values and with a clear sense of purpose and integrity between inner and outer. But there will always be a paradox in his life. There is "Estrus on the ground" in community settings. Then there is "Estrus in the circle of privilege," where he is often and still the only African American in the room or on the stage. Yet it is part of his calling to go places where change needs to occur and his voice needs to be heard, where change is longed for and his voice can be a catalyst for hopeful, human engagement.

Good questions work on us, we don't work on them. They are not a project to be completed but a doorway opening onto greater depth of understanding, actions that will take us into being more fully alive.
—Peter Block

The Courage to Leave Well

Greg Simmons was thirty-four years old when he became the CEO of MetaStar, Inc. The organization focuses on health care quality improvement, mainly through providing collaborative learning and technical assistance. After devoting himself and his career to one place for nearly forty years, he is now preparing to retire in 2020.

"I'm going to continue to need courage to understand what my important role is in the last few years of career, and keep my eye on the ball, if you will, creating a strong and seamless transition to the next leadership for the organization."

How to "leave well" while leading well is important to Greg. "I was feeling a little uneasy that I'm not as in touch with some of the day-to-day details of our contracts and projects as I once was, maybe ten years ago or more. I wanted to make sure that in my remaining years here, I was really being of value to the organization."

He had to work on sorting out things his true self already knew. Greg had the chance in one of our programs to receive open, honest questions focused on helping him get clarity about his dilemma: *What have you done in your career that you think most contributed to how the organization is now? Of those things, what do you think are the most important to carry forward? Who's going to do that? How's that going to happen?*

"What's important for me is not the day-to-day tasks and checking of the boxes in the contracts, and grants, and so forth, but it's this preparing to hand it off to other people."

Greg told me that he got a lot of peace out of the process of questioning how to transition out of his leadership role at the company. "My role really does need to change to one of handing over this organism that's grown up and been created over the last four decades to a new generation."

Greg is now resolved to do what he can to make sure that the cultural aspects of his company have the greatest chance possible of persisting into the future. "The philosophy and the values that we've created over time have been the cornerstones of what we've been able to do as an organization. I think we're in pretty good shape that way. Obviously, I'm not going to be here anymore, so I won't be able to control that. I probably can't control it now," he added with a smile.

Relay

I thought
It was a marathon,
The work
That must be done.
I learned
It was a relay.

That changed everything.

—Judy Brown, *The Art and Spirit of Leadership*[1]

The Art and Practice of Skillful Transitions

Judy Brown knows that almost all of her work these days is a relay race, marked by baton passing to the next generation.

"The leadership development work I do is important work—preparing the next generation of stewards, who are linking leadership, learning, and creativity as a framework for sustainable change in their lives, organizations, and the world. It is not a time for winding down. In order to pass the baton to the next runner, you have to maintain momentum and rely on the practice and on your teammates. While the handoff is crucial, it is collaborative work."

As one leader passes the baton to the next, it's important to consider the light or shadow he or she leaves behind. A lack of internal awareness, readiness, or peace with the process can cast shadows. Have you ever noticed the very long shadow of tall trees or tall buildings at the end of the day, when the afternoon light is often most golden? Shadows can become helpful shade if the person leaving does so intentionally and artfully.

For leaders in organizations, and perhaps anyone, letting go means releasing one's inner assumptions, generalities, expectations, and demands that things have to be a certain way. Letting go means releasing what is no longer yours to carry. Your hands are free to discover something new to hold, and meanwhile enjoy being empty and free. "Get a grip" can leave your lexicon.

The decision to leave or stay in a job, in a relationship, in a place, has no right or wrong answer. Each decision is another on the never-ending journey toward a life of integrity.

"The opposite of right is not wrong, it's curious," Judy said. "That thought keeps coming back to me. When I give up being right, I have access to being curious."

The "courage to stay" isn't only about staying in your job. It can mean the courage to stay curious, willing to seek understanding by asking good questions. Willing to stay open to receiving hard questions instead of being defensive. It takes courage to stay true to yourself and stay true to others. It takes courage to stay in rough conversations, allowing the tensions to stretch open your heart and mind until you can see a way to move forward.

> Believe in what you do and think hard about what kind of change you want your work to make.

—Ceci Bastida, Latin singer/songwriter

The Courage to Stay True

Leaders like Dave, Estrus, and Greg stayed a long time in their roles, until they knew it was time to move on. Many of the leaders throughout this book are ones who have stayed in their organizations. Staying power comes from clarity around your commitments.

As Dave said, it's vital that enough change agents stay in—or go to—places where systems need reinventing. We can't all be or work for enlightened CEOs who are creating change from the top down.

Frederic Laloux once put it this way: "When middle managers yearn for change, I start by asking them: How badly do you want things to change? What risks are you prepared to take? How long do you plan to stay in your current position? Would you consider experimenting boldly? Do you have a 'shit umbrella' above your head so that you can continue to play the game as much as you must, but no more, and proceed to experiment with alternative behaviors within your sphere of control?"[2]

Whether for economic reasons or for one of countless others, it's not always possible to leave a position. So if you know you must stay in a place that is not quite what you hoped for, but you have energy to make some change, here's another question to ask yourself: *What's the thing I can't not do?*

Fortifying for Your Journey Ahead

You can't help but be transformed, turned nearly inside out, by your leadership journey on the Möbius strip, by the lifelong journey toward becoming your true self. Thomas Merton writes, "There is in us an instinct for newness, for renewal, for a liberation of creative power. We seek to awaken in ourselves a force that really changes our lives from within. And yet the same instinct tells us that this change is a recovery of that which is deepest, most original, most personal in ourselves."[3]

We have a custom at the end of programs, retreats, and team meetings to do a closing round during which people share heartfelt thoughts. And when I ended my interviews with leaders, I would often ask, *What would you say you need courage for next?*

On that grace note, then, we share a few wishes for your continuing Courage Way journey: May your lay-awake nights as a leader be spent in conversation with your true self. May you get out of bed every morning with something fulfilling ahead. May you be fortified by people you love wholly and trust, and may you fortify them in return.

And at the end of your day, especially the hard ones, may you trust that your work is worthwhile, and may you hear the song in your heart.

Night Song of the World

He stood outside the horse truck, waiting for Mogador to come back and he began to whistle. Across the field the men had taken down the sides of the tent and were moving about in dim light under the top, picking up trunks, ropes and equipment and packing it away. He began to whistle a tune from the depths of his soul; he had never heard it before but he recognized it as a form of the song his soul had always been singing, a song he had been singing since the beginning of the world, a song of return. It was as though he stood in a dark corner of the universe and whistled softly, between his teeth, and the far stars were attentive, as though he whistled and waves far off could hear him, as though he had discovered a strain at least of the night song of the world.

—Robert Lax, *The Circus of the Sun*[4]

Notes

Introduction: Why Courage?

[1] After facilitators are trained in the Circle of Trust® approach by the Center for Courage & Renewal, they are authorized to design and deliver custom programs to fit the needs of their own community. One bright-spot example is the Courage to Lead for Nonprofit Leaders program, created by facilitators Ken Saxon and Kim Stokely in Southern California. By its ninth year in 2017, it had grown to one hundred forty alumni who stay connected as a local community of practice. See www.leading-from-within.org/courage-to-lead-2/.

[2] William Stafford, "A Ritual to Read to Each Other," in *The Way It Is: New and Selected Poems* (Minneapolis: Graywolf Press, 1998), 75.

[3]   Nik Gowing and Chris Langdon, *Thinking the Unthinkable: A New Imperative for Leadership in the Digital Age; An Interim Report* (London: Chartered Institute of Management Accountants, 2016), http://thinkunthinkable.org/.

[4]   "The Impact of Stress in the Classroom," Center for Embodied Wisdom (n.d.), https://www.cen treforembodiedwisdom.com/impa ct-of-stress-in-the-classroom/; Holly E. Mullin, "The Stress Response: Fight, Flight, Freeze, Feed & Fornicate," *Elephant Journal,* August 16, 2013, https ://www.elephantjournal.com/201 3/08/the-stress-response-fightflig htfreezefeed-fornicate-holly-e-mu llin/..

[5]   Alistair Smith, *The Brain's Behind It: New Knowledge About the Brain and Learning* (Stafford, UK: Network Educational Press, Ltd., 2002), 181.

[6]   Besides fight, flight, freeze, and flock, other stress responses beginning with the letter *F* appear in research literature and

online: fawn, feed, and feign. Then there's using the "F-word" itself, which is a sure sign of stress. Forgiveness would count as a positive response.

[7] Gregory M. Reichberg, *Thomas Aquinas on War and Peace* (Cambridge, UK: Cambridge University Press, 2017), 84–85.

[8] Monica C. Worline, "Valor," in *Character Strengths and Virtues: A Handbook and Classification,* ed. Christopher Peterson and Martin Seligman (New York: Oxford University Press, 2004), 213–228.

[9] Malala Yousafzai, speech before the United Nations General Assembly, July 12, 2013. Full text of speech: http://www.inde pendent.co.uk/news/world/asia/t he-full-text-malala-yousafzai-deli vers-defiant-riposte-to-taliban-mi litants-with-speech-to-the-un-87 06606.html.

[10] Brené Brown's January 2011 TED Talk, "The Power of Vulnerability," has been viewed over six million times; it

launched several more books and ongoing research. Available on YouTube, 20:49, posted by TED January 3, 2011, https://www.youtube.com/watch?v=iCvmsMzlF7o.

[11] Ryan McKelley, "Unmasking Masculinity—Helping Boys Become Connected Men," TEDxUWLaCrosse. Available on YouTube, 18:20, posted by TEDx November 26, 2013, https://www.youtube.com/watch?v=LbdnjqEoiXA.

[12] John O'Donohue, "For a New Beginning," in *To Bless the Space Between Us* (New York: Doubleday, 2008), 14.

[13] Mary Ann Radmacher, *Live Boldly* (San Francisco: Conari Press, 2008), 4.

[14] Monica C. Worline, "Dancing the Cliff Edge: The Role of Courage in Social Life" (PhD dissertation, University of Michigan, 2004); Monica C. Worline, "Courage in Organizations: An Integrative Review of 'the Difficult Virtue,'" in *Handbook of Positive*

Organizational Scholarship, ed. Kim S. Cameron and Gretchen M. Spreitzer (New York: Oxford University Press, 2011), 304–315.

[15]   Monica C. Worline and Jane E. Dutton, *Awakening Compassion at Work* (Oakland, CA: Berrett-Koehler, 2017), 57.

[16]   Allison Rimm, "To Guide Difficult Conversations, Try Using Compassion," *Harvard Business Review,* June 19, 2013, https://hbr.org/2013/06/to-guide-difficult-conversation.

Chapter 1: What Is the Courage Way?

[1]   The Center for Courage & Renewal has trademarked the name Circle of Trust® approach to define this specific collection of principles and practices. This designation is for use only by facilitators who have been prepared by the Center. A circle of trust (lowercase) is the experience itself of intentional

group dialogue, which can take place even in a group of two people.

[2]   Wendell Barry, "The Wild Geese," in *Collected Poems 1957–1982* (New York: North Point Press, 1998).

Chapter 2: The Inner Work of Leadership

[1]   Parker J. Palmer, *The Courage to Teach,* 20th anniv. ed. (San Francisco: Jossey-Bass, 2017), 11.

[2]   Named for August Ferdinand Möbius, the nineteenth-century German mathematician who discovered it.

[3]   Diana Chapman Walsh, interview by Courage & Renewal facilitators Rick Jackson and Diane Rawlins, Seattle, WA, August 9, 2006.

[4]   William Ayot, *E-mail from the Soul: New and Selected Leadership Poems* (Chepstow, South East Wales: Sleeping Mountain Press, 2014), 13.

[5]   Ibid.

Chapter 3: Have You Met Your True Self?

[1] C. Otto Scharmer, *Theory U,* 2nd ed. (Oakland, CA: Berrett-Koehler, 2016), 22.

[2] John O'Donohue, "The Inner History of a Day," in *To Bless the Space Between Us* (New York: Doubleday, 2008), 161.

[3] William Stafford, "A Ritual to Read to Each Other," in *The Way It Is: New and Selected Poems* (Minneapolis: Graywolf Press, 1998), 75.

[4] Marie-Louise von Franz, *Shadow and Evil in Fairy Tales* (Boston: Shambhala, 1995), 3.

[5] William Ayot, excerpt from "An Away-Day with the Shadow," in *E-mail from the Soul: New and Selected Leadership Poems* (Chepstow, South East Wales: Sleeping Mountain Press, 2014), 102.

[6] Marie-Louise von Franz, *Shadow and Evil in Fairy Tales* (Boston: Shambhala, 1995), 5.

[7]   Parker J. Palmer, *Let Your Life Speak* (San Francisco: Jossey-Bass, 2000), 86.

Chapter 4: Courage Takes Trust

[1]   "The Parable of the Trapeze—Danaan Parry," YouTube video, 6:06, posted by Arocany April 7, 2012, https://youtube/HWvV5N4`hOGc. Words by Danaan Parry, *Warriors of the Hear* (Bainbridge Island, WA: Earth Stewards Network, 1991), 83. Also see http://www.earthstewards.org/ESN-Trapeze.asp

[2]   Anthony S. Bryk and Barbara Schneider, *Trust in Schools: A Core Resource for Improvement* (New York: Russell Sage Foundation, 2002), 22–26, 122–124; Anthony S. Bryk, Penny Bender Sebring, Elaine Allensworth, John Q. Easton, and Stuart Luppescu, *Organizing Schools for Improvement: Lessons from Chicago* (Chicago: University of Chicago Press,

2010). This research also included colleagues at the Urban Institute and the Alfred P. Sloan Center on Parents, Children and Work, University of Chicago, and the Consortium on Chicago School Research. In chapter 2 of *Trust in Schools,* the authors differentiate relational trust from organic and contractual trust, and describe a theory grounded in philosophy, political science, economics, and organization behavior.

[3] Catherine Gewertz, "'Trusting' School Community Linked to Student Gains," *Education Week,* October 16, 2002, http://www.edweek.org/ew/articles/2002/10/16/07trust.h22.html.

[4] Pamela Seigle, Lisa Sankowski, and Chip Wood, facilitators of the Center for Courage & Renewal, brought their own professional expertise and passions to work with collaborators and researchers to develop and pilot practical applications for improving

relational trust in schools. Leading Together: Building Adult Community in Schools was a pilot program that brought together principals and teacher leaders to experience reflective practices and protocols that can be facilitated in faculty meetings, grade-level meetings, child study teams, parent meetings, and classrooms. For more information, see www.couragere newal.org/leadingtogether.

[5]   Sara E. Rimm-Kaufman, Micela Leis, and Carol Paxton, *Innovating Together to Improve the Adult Community in Schools: Results from a Two-Year Study of the Initial Implementation of Leading Together* (Charlottesville: University of Virginia, June 26, 2014), www.c ouragerenewal.org/PDFs/UVA_Le adingTogether_July_11_2014_Fin al_Full_Report.pdf.

[6]   Bryk and Schneider, *Trust in Schools,* 23.

[7]   Nik Gowing and Chris Langdon, *Thinking the Unthinkable: A New*

Imperative for Leadership in the Digital Age; An Interim Report (London: Chartered Institute of Management Accountants, 2016), http://thinkunthinkable.org.

[8]   Bryk and Schneider, *Trust in Schools,* 137.

[9]   Ibid., 26.

Chapter 5: Reflection in Community

[1]   "The Writing Worm," *Island,* January 2017: 5, https://cdn.sh opify.com/s/files/1/0695/3129/fil es/Chatter_matters_PDF_publicat ion_V2.pdf?11691364722338020 443.

[2]   Rosie Martin, "Cochineal," *Transportation Press,* January 14, 2015, https://transportationpres s.net/tag/rosie-martin/.

[3]   Rosalie "Rosie" Martin received the 2017 Tasmanian Australian of the Year to honor her pioneering work in the teaching of language, literacy, and social communication to adults, including prisoners. See https://

www.australianoftheyear.org.au/
honour-roll/?view=fullView&recipi
entID=1824.

[4]   The Circle of Security method is
        unrelated to the Courage &
        Renewal Circle of Trust approach,
        although it applies similar
        concepts. See Circle of Security
        International, Spokane, WA, htt
        ps://www.circleofsecurityinternat
        ional.com.

[5]   Rainer Maria Rilke, *Letters to a
        Young Poet,* trans. M.D. Herter
        (New York: Norton, 1993), 59.

[6]   Parker J. Palmer, *A Hidden
        Wholeness* (San Francisco:
        Jossey-Bass, 2004), 64.

[7]   Ibid., 60.

[8]   Nancy Olson, "Three Ways That
        Handwriting with a Pen Positively
        Affects Your Brain," Forbes.com,
        May 15, 2016, https://www.forb
        es.com/sites/nancyolson/2016/05
        /15/three-ways-that-writing-with
        -a-pen-positively-affects-your-bra
        in/#37557ecc5705.

[9]   Rosalie Martin, "Introduction,"
        Island, January 2017: 3, https:/

/islandmag.com/pages/chatter-matters.

[10]   The Center for Courage & Renewal is a founding partner in the IHI 100 Million Healthier Lives initiative, which inspired these phrases about leading for change. It is an unprecedented collaboration of change agents across sectors to create an equitable health and wellbeing system. See https://www.100m lives.org/.

[11]   Parker J. Palmer, *Healing the Heart of Democracy* (San Francisco: Jossey-Bass, 2011), 45.

Chapter 6: The Courage to Care for True Self

[1]   Every year since 2002, the Accreditation Council for Graduate Medical Education (ACGME) has honored ten physicians with the Parker J. Palmer Courage to Teach Award for finding innovative ways to teach residents and to provide

quality health care while remaining connected to the initial impulse to care for others. It also annually confers Parker J. Palmer Courage to Lead awards to institutional officials who have demonstrated strong leadership and astute resource management and have encouraged innovation and improvement in residency programs and their sponsoring institutions. ACGME is the accreditation organization for approximately ten thousand post-MD medical residency and fellowship training programs in the United States. See http://www.acgme.org/What-We-Do/Initiatives/Awards/Parker-J-Palmer-Courage-to-Teach-Award.

[2]   Mandy Oaklander, "Life/Support: Inside the Movement to Save the Mental Health of American's Doctors," *TIME,* September 7–14, 2015: 42–51.

[3]   Nicole M. Cranley, Christopher J.L. Cunningham, and Mukta Panda, "Understanding Time Use, Stress and Recovery Practices

Among Early Career Physicians: An Exploratory Study," *Psychology, Health & Medicine* 21, no.3 (2016): 362–367, doi: 10.1080/13548506.2015.106167 5.

[4]   Thomas Merton, *Conjectures of a Guilty Bystander* (New York: Image Doubleday, 1989), 86.

[5]   Parker J. Palmer, *The Courage to Teach* (San Francisco: Jossey-Bass, 2007), 205.

Chapter 7: The Courage to Answer Your Calling

[1]   Parker J. Palmer, *Let Your Life Speak* (San Francisco: Jossey-Bass, 2000), 4.

[2]   Bryan J. Dik and Ryan D. Duffy, *Make Your Job a Calling: How the Psychology of Vocation Can Change Your Life at Work* (West Conshohocken, PA: Templeton Press, 2012).

[3]   Michael G. Pratt, Camille Pradies, and Douglas A. Lepisto, "Doing Well, Doing Good and Doing With: Organizational Practices for

Effectively Cultivating Meaningful Work," in *Purpose and Meaning in the Workplace,* ed. Bryan Dik, Zinta Byrne, and Michael Steger (Washington, DC: American Psychological Association, 2013), 173–191.

[4]   John Paul Lederach, *The Moral Imagination* (New York: Oxford University Press, 2005), 165.

Chapter 8: The Courage to Question and Listen

[1]   Dawna Markova, "Thinking Ourselves Home," in *Living the Questions: Essays Inspired by the Work and Life of Parker J. Palmer,* ed. Sam Intrator (San Francisco: Jossey-Bass, 2005), 65.

[2]   Robert Kegan and Lisa Laskow Lahey, *An Everyone Culture* (Boston: Harvard Business Review Press, 2016).

[3]   Frederic Laloux, *Reinventing Organizations* (Brussels: Nelson Parker, 2014).

[4]   Ian Leslie, *Curious* (New York: Basic Books, 2014), xiv.

Chapter 9: The Courage to Hold Tension in Life-Giving Ways

[1]   Parker J. Palmer, *To Know as We Are Known: A Spirituality of Education* (San Francisco: Harper & Row, 1983).

[2]   Michael S. Schneider, *A Beginner's Guide to Constructing the Universe: The Mathematical Archetypes of Nature, Art and Science* (New York: HarperCollins, 1994), 39. A mathematics teacher, Schneider wrote this book to illuminate the principles of nature and philosophy inherent in geometry, in large part because as a child he dreaded the dry, irrelevant lessons, and wishes he'd known the magic behind math. In his chapter on the numeral three, he has a paragraph on Perceval—the only one of three

knights to find the grail, which scholars and Jungians agree is a symbol of self-knowledge.

Chapter 10: The Courage to Choose Wisely

[1]   Dawna Markova, *I Will Not Die an Unlived Life* (Berkeley, CA: Conari Press, 2000), 1.

[2]   Howard Thurman, "The Sound of the Genuine," baccalaureate address at Spelman College, May 4, 1980, as edited by Jo Moore Stewart in *Spelman Messenger* 96, no.4 (Summer 1980): 14–15. Reprinted in "Crossings Reflection #4," University of Indiana, http://eip.uindy.edu/crossings/publications/reflection4.pdf.

Chapter 11: The Courage to Connect and Trust in Each Other

[1]   Peter Block, *Community: The Structure of Belonging* (Oakland, CA: Berrett-Koehler, 2008), 155.

[2]   Sherry K. Watt, *Designing Transformative Multicultural Initiatives: Theoretical Foundations, Practical Applications, and Facilitator Considerations* (Sterling, VA: Stylus Publishing, 2015), 17–21.

[3]   Ibid., 20.

[4]   Parker J. Palmer, *A Hidden Wholeness* (San Francisco: Jossey-Bass, 2004), 65.

[5]   Ibid., 65.

[6]   Brian Arao and Kristi Clemens, "From Safe Spaces to Brave Spaces: A New Way to Frame Dialogue Around Diversity and Social Justice," in *The Art of Effective Facilitation,* ed. Lisa A. Landreman (Sterling, VA: Stylus, 2013), 135–149.

[7]   Ibid., 136.

[8]   For more about The Welcome Table project, see http://winteri nstitute.org/community-relations /the-welcome-table/.

[9]   To learn about the origins of the Where I'm From exercise, see poet George Ella Lyons's web

page http://www.georgeellalyon.com/where.html.

Chapter 12: The Courage to Stay or to Leave

[1] Judy Brown, *The Art and Spirit of Leadership* (Bloomington, IL: Trafford, 2012), 221.

[2] Frederic Laloux, in group conversation in Parker Palmer's living room, Madison, WI, January 27, 2015. Also see his book, *Reinventing Organizations* (Brussels: Nelson Parker, 2014).

[3] Thomas Merton, *Love and Living,* eds. Naomi Burton Stone and Brother Patrick Hart (Orlando, FL: Houghton Mifflin Harcourt, 2002), 196.

[4] Robert Lax, *The Circus of the Sun* (New York: Journeyman Books, 1960).

Quote Sources

Preface

Le Guin, Ursula K. *Words Are My Matter: Writings About Life and Books, 2000–2016, with a Journal of a Writer's Week.* Easthampton, MA: Small Beer Press, 2016, 50.

Introduction: Why Courage?

Angelou, Maya. Interview in *USA TODAY,* March 5, 1988. https://www.us atoday.com/story/news/nation-now/201 4/05/28/maya-angelou-quotes/9663257/

May, Rollo. *The Courage to Create.* New York: W.W. Norton & Company, Inc., 1975, 2.

Palmer, Parker J. *Let Your Life Speak.* San Francisco: Jossey-Bass, 2000, 93.

Chapter 1: What Is the Courage Way?

Helsing, Deborah, Annie Howell, Robert Kegan, and Lisa Lahey. "Putting the 'Development' in Professional

Development." *Harvard Educational Review* 78, no.3 (Fall 2008): 437–465.

Palmer, Parker J. *Let Your Life Speak.* San Francisco: Jossey-Bass, 2000, 78. [Our complicity in world making..."]

_____. *Healing the Heart of Democracy.* San Francisco: Jossey-Bass, 2011, 15. ["At the deepest levels..."]

_____. *A Hidden Wholeness.* San Francisco: Jossey-Bass, 2004, 10–11. ["If we are willing..."]

Chapter 2: The Inner Work of Leadership

Ayot, William. *E-mail from the Soul: New and Selected Leadership Poems.* Chepstow, South East Wales: Sleeping Mountain Press, 2014, 13.

Havel, Václav. Speech delivered to a joint meeting of the US Congress on February 21, 1990. In *The Art of the Impossible,* trans. Paul Wilson. New York: Knopf, 1997, 17–18. Discussed in Parker J. Palmer, *Let Your Life Speak.* San Francisco: Jossey-Bass, 2000, 75.

Palmer, Parker J. *A Hidden Wholeness.* San Francisco: Jossey-Bass,

2004, 16–17. ["Is this person the same..."]

_____. "Thirteen Ways of Looking at Community." *The Inner Edge,* August/September 1998. ["We were created..."]

Senge, Peter, Hal Hamilton, and John Kania. "The Dawn of System Leadership." *Stanford Social Innovation Review,* Winter 2015: 26–33.

Chapter 3: Have You Met Your True Self?

Palmer, Parker J. Adapted from *The Courage to Teach.* San Francisco: Jossey-Bass, 2007, 4. ["But seldom if ever..."]

_____. *The Courage to Teach.* San Francisco: Jossey-Bass, 2007, 14. ["By choosing integrity..."]

_____. *Let Your Life Speak.* San Francisco: Jossey-Bass, 2000, 78. ["A good leader is intensely aware..."]

Popova, Maria. "On the Soul-Sustaining Necessity of Resisting Self-Comparison and Fighting Cynicism: A Commencement Address." *Brain Pickings,* May 16, 2016. https://www.b

rainpickings.org/2016/05/16/annenberg-commencement/.

Whitman, Walt. "Song of Myself." In *Leaves of Grass.* Final "Death-Bed" ed., 1891–2. David McKay, 1892. Also see www.poetryfoundation.org/poems/45477/song-of-myself-1892-version.

Chapter 4: Courage Takes Trust

Nouwen, Henri J.M. *Reaching Out.* New York: Doubleday, 1975, 74.

Scott-Maxwell, Florida. *The Measure of My Days.* New York: Alfred P. Knopf, 1979, 42.

Vanier, Jean. *Becoming Human.* Mahwah, NJ: Paulist Press, 1998, 83.

Chapter 5: Reflection in Community

Palmer, Parker J. *A Hidden Wholeness.* San Francisco: Jossey-Bass, 2004, 55. ["Our lives as leaders..."]

_____. "Introduction." In *Leading from Within: Poetry That Sustains the Courage to Lead,* ed. Sam M. Intrator and Megan Scribner. San Francisco

Jossey-Bass, 2007. ["We have much to learn...]

Petzet, Heinrich Wiegand. "Foreword." In Rainer Maria Rilke, *Letters on Cezanne,* ed. Clara Rilke, trans. Joel Agee. New York: International Publishing, 1978, xxii.

Schön, Donald A. "Knowing-in-Action: The New Scholarship Requires a New Epistemology," *Change: The Magazine of Higher Learning* 27, no.6 (November/December 1995): 27–34.

Chapter 6: The Courage to Care for True Self

Merton, Thomas. *Conjectures of a Guilty Bystander.* New York: Image Doubleday, 1989, 86.

Palmer, Parker J. *Let Your Life Speak.* San Francisco: Jossey-Bass, 2000, 30–31. ["Self-care is never a selfish act..."]

_____. *The Courage to Teach.* San Francisco: Jossey-Bass, 2007, 211. ["I must wrap my life around this question..."]

_____. *A Hidden Wholeness.* San Francisco: Jossey-Bass, 2004, 82–83. ["The deeper our faith..."]

Chapter 7: The Courage to Answer Your Calling

Albright, Madeline. "Foreword." In *Leading from Within: Poetry That Sustains the Courage to Lead,* ed. Sam M. Intrator and Megan Scribner. San Francisco: Jossey-Bass, 2007, xvi.

Berends, Polly Berrien. *Coming to Life: Traveling the Spiritual Path in Everyday Life.* New York: HarperCollins, 1990, 8.

Mandela, Nelson. In *Mandela: The Life of Nelson Mandela,* ed. Rod Green. New York: Thomas Dunne Books, 2012, 33.

Millman, Debbie. "Fail Safe." In *Look Both Ways: Illustrated Essays on the Intersection of Life and Design.* Cincinnati, OH: HOW Books, 2009, 191.

Palmer, Parker J. *Let Your Life Speak.* San Francisco: Jossey-Bass, 2000, 25.

Thurman, Howard. Quoted in Gil Bailie, *Violence Unveiled: Humanity at the Crossroads.* New York: Crossroad Publishing Company, 1995, xv.

Chapter 8: The Courage to Question and Listen

Markova, Dawna. "Thinking Ourselves Home." In *Living the Questions: Essays Inspired by the Work and Life of Parker J. Palmer,* ed. Sam Intrator. San Francisco: Jossey-Bass, 2005, 65.

Palmer, Parker J. *A Hidden Wholeness.* San Francisco: Jossey-Bass, 2004, 39.

Tippett, Krista. *Becoming Wise.* New York: Penguin Press, 2016, 30.

Chapter 9: The Courage to Hold Tension in Life-Giving Ways

Frankl, Victor. *Man's Search for Meaning.* Boston: Beacon Press, 1959, 75.

Palmer, Parker J. *The Courage to Teach.* 20th anniv. ed. San Francisco: Jossey-Bass, 2017, 87. ["The tension always feels difficult..."]

_____. *Healing the Heart of Democracy.* San Francisco: Jossey-Bass, 2011, xx. ["We engage in creative tension-holding..."]

_____. *A Hidden Wholeness.* San Francisco: Jossey-Bass, 2004, 127. ["We must find a way to live..."]

Chapter 10: The Courage to Choose Wisely

May, Rollo. *The Courage to Create.* New York: W.W. Norton & Company, Inc., 1975, 5.

Palmer, Parker J. *A Hidden Wholeness.* San Francisco: Jossey-Bass, 2004, 45.

Thurman, Howard. "The Sound of the Genuine." Baccalaureate address at Spelman College, May 4, 1980, as edited by Jo Moore Stewart in *Spelman Messenger 96,* no.4 (Summer 1980): 14–15. Reprinted in "Crossings Reflection #4," University of Indiana, http://eip.uindy.edu/crossings/publications/reflection4.pdf.

Chapter 11: The Courage to Connect and Trust in Each Other

The Root Staff. "Maya Angelou's Words That Spoke to All Our Lives." *Root,* May 28, 2014. http://www.theroo t.com/maya-angelou-s-words-that-spoke -to-all-our-lives-1790875890.

Buechner, Frederick. *Beyond Words: Daily Readings in the ABCs of Faith.* New York: HarperCollins, 2004, 139.

Palmer, Parker J. *Healing the Heart of Democracy.* San Francisco: Jossey-Bass, 2011, 99. ["In the company of strangers..."]

_____. *A Hidden Wholeness.* San Francisco: Jossey-Bass, 2004, 65. ["You cannot gather people and say..."]

Stewart, Dafina-Lazarus. "Language of Appeasement." *Inside Higher Ed,* March 30, 2017. https://www.insidehig hered.com/views/2017/03/30/colleges-n eed-language-shift-not-one-you-think-es say.

Watt, Sherry K. *Designing Transformative Multicultural Initiatives: Theoretical Foundations, Practical*

Applications, and Facilitator Considerations. Sterling, VA: Stylus, 2015, 19.

Zhuang, Justin. "Design History 101: Quietly Beautiful Work by the Illustrator Who Drew the Four Seasons Logo; A Search for the Mid-Century 'Soft Modernism' of Emil Antonucci." *AIGA Eye on Design,* April 9, 2015, http://Ey eondesign.Aiga.Org/Design-History-101-Quietly-Beautiful-Work-By-Illustrator-Wh o-Drew-Four-Seasons-Logo/.

Chapter 12: The Courage to Stay or to Leave

Nunez, Vivian. "Important Career Lessons Ceci Bastida Learned by Being a Latin Independent Artist." Women@Forbes, December 14, 2016. https://www.forbes.com/sites/viviannun ez/2016/12/14/5-important-career-lesso ns-ceci-bastida-learned-by-being-a-latin -independent-artist/

Schepici, Kristin. "A Conversation with Peter Block." Linkage.com, January 12, 2011. http://blog.linkageinc.com/bl og/a-conversation-with-peter-block-orga nizational-development-legend-and-recip ient-of-linkage%E2%80%99s-lifetime-achievement-award/

Walsh, Diana Chapman. "Potbound" (final stanza). She wrote this unpublished poem March 5, 1990, at a retreat in Taos, New Mexico, three years before she left Harvard to become the president of Wellesley College.

Recommended Reading

Books by the Center for Courage & Renewal

Living the Questions: Essays Inspired by the Work and Life of Parker J. Palmer, Sam M. Intrator, Editor

Poetry Anthologies with Leader Reflections, by Sam M. Intrator and Megan Scribner, Editors

Leading from Within

Teaching with Heart

Teaching with Fire

See our website for an extensive list of books written by Courage & Renewal Facilitators: couragerenewal.org/books-by-facilitators

Books by Parker J. Palmer

The Courage to Teach
Healing the Heart of Democracy
A Hidden Wholeness
Let Your Life Speak
The Promise of Paradox
The Active Life
To Know as We Are Known
The Company of Strangers
The Heart of Higher Education
(with Arthur Zajonc and Megan Scribner)

Gratitudes

> For all that has been, thanks.
> For all that will be, yes.
> —Dag Hammarskjöld

So many inspiring leaders are bringing their whole hearts to their work and making a difference in the world because of the generosity of our incredible supporters of the Center for Courage & Renewal. Deep gratitude to the individuals and foundations who believed this experiment in integrity was too true to fail and too good to limit, who gave of their time, treasure, and talent.

To all the leaders whose stories appear on these pages, and everyone whose stories are between the lines, too. Thank you for being the courageous ones who are making a difference every day by connecting your soul and role.

In *Let Your Life Speak,* Parker Palmer writes, "Truth is an eternal conversation about things that matter, conducted with passion and discipline. Truth cannot possibly be found in the conclusions of the conversation, because the conclusions keep changing."

My great gratitude to Parker, for being in this conversation with me through your wise words and true friendship. Because of you I have the practice of paradox and Quaker Zen koans, like the one quoted here, for every occasion! Great gratitude to Marcy Jackson and Rick Jackson for your perspective, wisdom, and incredible hearts as cofounders and senior fellows of the Center for Courage & Renewal. Special thanks to Terry Chadsey, the executive director who said we should write this book and then let me do it; your leadership gifts are in these pages as well. If it were not for these four leaders who founded and stewarded the Center all these years, there would not have been a Courage Way story to tell.

Heartfelt gratitude to all the wonderful Courage & Renewal facilitators and board members who make all this possible, too—your passion and gifts planted the seeds that grew, blossomed, and are now bearing such significant fruit. Thank you so much for talking through ideas and sharing your experience so that I could see the big picture over time and place, as well as the details up close.

It's truly the people we work with who make all the difference. A deep bow of gratitude to my editor, Sheryl Fullerton, for your wise counsel, encouragement, and patience with my process, and extra-large thanks for connecting us with the great people at Berrett-Koehler. Thank you, Erin Lane, for the gift of your editing eyes and writer's heart. Much gratitude goes to Marianne Houston, Barb Hummel, Ken Saxon, and Janet Smith for introducing me to amazing leaders.

Thanks to our new executive director, Terasa Cooley, whose leadership will continue creating a container for the larger story to unfold. And to the Center for Courage & Renewal staff through the years—you know who you are—thanks for showing up daily with your whole selves and keeping it real. I am grateful for all the conversations we've had!

To family and friends whose love makes each day worthwhile. You kept me going: Brian Casey, Wil Vickroy,

Dianne Dickerson, Moira Gray, Kathy and Grace Matsey, and Kristen Peters. Thank you to my sister, Jenéne Francis, and my parents, Rena Francis and Jeff Francis, for all your love since day one.

The universe conspires in marvelous ways, through people who deliver gifts at the perfect moment, rarely knowing their part. Gratitude goes to Carrie Newcomer and Alan Claassen for your songs; to Steve Georgiou, Joe Sarnelle, and Marcia Kelly for connecting me to Robert Lax; to Maria Popova for curating so much wisdom with your Brain Pickings; and to Denise Levertov for inspiring me with your poetry.

CENTER FOR

Courage
&Renewal

The Center for Courage & Renewal is a nonprofit organization that works to create a more just, compassionate, and healthy world by nurturing personal and professional integrity and the courage to act on it. Founded in 1997 by author, activist, and educator Parker J. Palmer, the Center's approach was initially created to renew and sustain educators, and today brings the Circle of Trust® approach to individuals, organizations, and communities across a range of professions. Through its network of nearly three hundred Courage & Renewal facilitators across the globe, the Center offers online resources and in-person retreats and programs, including facilitator-led retreats, workshops, team coaching, customized consulting, speaking presentations, and program series. "Touchstone" is a new initiative focused on senior executives who want to bring authentic, visionary leadership to their organizations.

Center for Courage & Renewal
1402 Third Avenue, Suite 925,
Seattle, WA 98101
206–466–2055|web@couragerenew
al.org

Discover more at www.CourageRe
newal.org
www.CourageWay.org
www.TouchstoneTrustedLeader.org

About the Coauthor

Shelly L. Francis has been the marketing and communications director at the Center for Courage & Renewal since mid-2012. Before coming to the Center, Shelly directed trade marketing and publicity for multimedia publisher Sounds True, Inc. Her career has spanned international program management, web design, corporate communications, trade journals, and software manuals. The common thread has been bringing to light "best-kept secrets"—technology, services, resources, ideas—while bringing people together to facilitate collective impact and good work. Shelly is the author of *Damocles' Wife,* her memoir on cancer caregiving and long-term survival.

❋ Berrett–Koehler
BK̄ Publishers

Berrett-Koehler is an independent publisher dedicated to an ambitious mission: Connecting people and ideas to create a world that works for all.

We believe that the solutions to the world's problems will come from all of us, working at all levels: in our organizations, in our society, and in our own lives. Our BK Business books help people make their organizations more humane, democratic, diverse, and effective (we don't think there's any contradiction there). Our BK Currents books offer pathways to creating a more just, equitable, and sustainable society. Our BK Life books help people create positive change in their lives and align their personal practices with their aspirations for a better world.

All of our books are designed to bring people seeking positive change together around the ideas that empower them to see and shape the world in a new way.

And we strive to practice what we preach. At the core of our approach is

Stewardship, a deep sense of responsibility to administer the company for the benefit of all of our stakeholder groups including authors, customers, employees, investors, service providers, and the communities and environment around us. Everything we do is built around this and our other key values of quality, partnership, inclusion, and sustainability.

This is why we are both a B-Corporation and a California Benefit Corporation—a certification and a for-profit legal status that require us to adhere to the highest standards for corporate, social, and environmental performance.

We are grateful to our readers, authors, and other friends of the company who consider themselves to be part of the BK Community. We hope that you, too, will join us in our mission.

A BK Business Book

We hope you enjoy this BK Business book. BK Business books pioneer new leadership and management practices and socially responsible approaches to business. They are designed to provide you with groundbreaking and practical tools to transform your work and organizations while upholding the triple bottom line of people, planet, and profits. High-five!

To find out more, visit www.bkconn ection.com.

Berrett–Koehler
BK Publishers

Connecting people and ideas
to create a world that works for all

Dear Reader,

Thank you for picking up this book and joining our worldwide community of Berrett-Koehler readers. We share ideas that bring positive change into people's lives, organizations, and society.

To welcome you, we'd like to offer you a free e-book. You can pick from among twelve of our bestselling books by entering the promotional code **BKP92E** here: http://www.bkconnection.com/welcome.

When you claim your free e-book, we'll also send you a copy of our e-newsletter, the *BK Communiqué.* Although you're free to unsubscribe, there are many benefits to sticking around. In every issue of our newsletter you'll find

- A free e-book
- Tips from famous authors
- Discounts on spotlight titles
- Hilarious insider publishing news

- A chance to win a prize for answering a riddle

Best of all, our readers tell us, "Your newsletter is the only one I actually read." So claim your gift today, and please stay in touch!

Sincerely,
Charlotte Ashlock
Steward of the BK Website

Questions? Comments? Contact me at bkcommunity@bkpub.com.

Certified

B

Corporation

bcorporation.net

A

Albright, Madeline, *169*

Antonucci, Emil, *240*

Arao, Brian, *257, 259*

Auden, W. H., *57*

'An Away-Day with the Shadow' (Ayot), *76*

Ayot, William,

An Everyone Culture (Kegan and Lahey), *195*

A Hidden Wholeness (Palmer), *206, 254, 255*

A Place Called Home (APCH), *154, 156, 167*

B

Barry, Wendell, *31*

Beloved Community vision, *274*

Berends, Polly, *149*

Bici Centro, *63*

Block, Peter, *247, 248, 279*

Bob and Mike's story,

on asking open, honest questions, *184, 186, 188, 218*

on gift of listening without fixing, *181, 182*

Boone, Jill,

how questions opened up options, *199, 201, 218*

showing courage during tense situations, *199, 201*

transforming conflict instead of managing it, *201, 203*

Bourgeois, Christine, *81*

Boyer, Dave,

having the course to start MCD, Inc., *269, 270, 272*
his commitment to sustainability and stewardship, *272*
work stress experienced by, *266*
brave spaces, *257, 259*
Brown, Judy, *57, 177, 281, 283*
Bryk, Anthony, *98, 100, 106*
Buechner, Frederick, *254*
burnout,
  Ed France's struggle with, *77, 79*
  Mukta Panda's struggle with, *129, 132*

C
calling,
  meaning of vocational, *162, 163*

neoclassical meaning of, *162*
Center for Courage & Renewal,
  annual reviews structured with open, honest questions at, *194*
  Circle of Trust approach of, *10, 12, 14, 17, 255*
  Courage & Renewal Academy for Leaders program of, *36*
  Courage to Lead for Nonprofit Leaders program of, *65*
  Courage to Lead retreats of, *98, 145*
  Courage to Teach retreats of, *98*
  Ed France's empowerment after completing series of, *81*

exploring 'what-if
' questions at the,
5, 7
presidential
election at, 210
Leading Together:
Building Adult
Community in
Schools program
of, 98, 100
Lynne Fiscus's
applications of
principles of, 85, 88,
89, 91, 93, 95
relational trust
framework
developed by, 98,
100
their work
grounded in core
value of love, 120
See also Courage
Way Palmer,
Parker J.;
touchstones,
change,
art and practice of
skillful transitions
and, 281, 283

courage to leave
and still love
during, 274, 276, 278
courage to leave
well and embrace,
279, 281
courage to stay
true and
embrace, 285
fortifying your
Courage Way
journey ahead
for, 285, 286
Chatter Matters
charity, 115
choosing wisely,
choosing to risk,
225, 227
FTE's courage to
renew and
reinvent itself, 227,
228, 230, 232, 234
Greg Eaton's
story on, 218, 221, 223
inner truth used
to guide our, 218
to renew and
reinvent, 227, 228,
230, 232, 234

A Rubric for Choosing with Integrity, *236, 238*
trusting the process of, *234, 236*
chutzpah–humility paradox, *114, 115, 117*
Circle of Trust,
Center for Courage & Renewal's work using, *12*
Parker Palmer on the, *10, 255*
participation in conversation is always by invitation, *17*
touchstones facilitating the, *12, 14*
See also touchstones,
Clemens, Kristi, *257, 259*
Communities of inquiry, *122, 124*
community,
building trust in the, *51, 53*
choosing with integrity by looking for, *236, 238*
Courage Way and significance of a supportive, *9, 119, 120*
designing spaces to connect, *245, 247, 248*
Ed France's work building the biking, *63, 65, 67, 68*
as a gift to be received, *48*
Greg Sunter on building trust and, *175*
Habits of the Heart on capacity to create, *232, 234*
leadership capacity to create and receive, *37, 39, 48, 49, 51*

as requiring careful and regular tending, *37, 39, 49*

Community Environmental Council (CEC), *245, 247, 248*

community reflective practice,
communities of inquiry as, *122, 124*
finding common ground with third things, *124, 126*
importance and benefits of, *119, 120*
solitudes as a, *120, 122*

compassion,
micro-shift of leadership, *39, 41, 46, 48*
See also the heart,

competence relational trust lens of, *104, 106*

traditional perspective of, *104*

confidentiality touchstone,
commit to and maintain confidentiality, *14*
protecting trustworthy space, *26, 27*

conflict,
holding tension response to, *196, 204, 206, 208, 210*
how we engage in problem solving in tense situations and, *196*
transforming it instead of managing, *201, 203*

connections,
creating trustworthy space for making, *12, 14, 15, 17, 19, 21, 22, 24, 26, 27, 29*

designing spaces for community, *245, 247, 248*

Lellene Rector's commitment to LGBTQ inclusivity and, *241, 243*

Susan Glisson's work building, *261, 263, 264, 265*

valuing otherness to make, *259*

welcoming all sorts of diversity and, *251, 252, 254*

conversations,
  asking open, honest questions, *14, 22, 24*

  Greg Sunter's use of questions to invite people into, *170, 173, 175, 177*

  Kate Sheppard's holding the tension of the moment opening space for, *208, 210*

no fixing touchstone guiding, *14, 21*

shared truth arising from within meaningful, *31*

truth touchstone guiding truthful, *14, 19, 21*

wonder touchstone guiding rough, *14, 21, 22*

courage,
  comes from true self, *7*

  exists in the spaces between us, *31*

  fortitude and, *285, 286*

  giving voice to, *169, 170*

  to leave and still love, *274, 276, 278*

  to 'leave well', *279, 281*

courageous leadership,
  based on bringing your full self to your work, *158, 160, 162*
  See also leadership,
courageous leadership metaphors,
  jumping from ten-meter diving platform, *36, 37*
  Möbius strip, *41, 42, 44, 46, 53, 108, 238, 285, 286*
courageous leader stories,
  Bob and Mike, *181, 182, 184, 186, 188, 218*
  Dave Boyer, *266, 269, 270, 272*
  Diana Chapman Walsh, *55, 57*
  Ed France, *58, 61, 63, 65, 67, 68, 72, 77, 79, 81*
  Estrus Tucker, *274, 276, 278*

Greg Eaton, *192, 194, 218, 221, 223, 225*
Greg Simmons, *279, 281*
Greg Sunter, *170, 173, 175, 177*
Jill Boone, *199, 201, 203, 218*
Jonathan Zeichner, *149, 152, 154, 156, 158, 162, 167, 169*
Judy Brown, *57, 177, 281, 283*
Kate Sheppard, *206, 208, 210, 218, 251*
Lallene Rector, *240, 241, 243, 257*
Lynne Fiscus, *84, 85, 88, 89, 91, 93, 95, 102, 104*
Mukta Panda, *129, 132, 135, 137, 138, 141*
Patrick Herson, *34, 36, 37, 39, 41, 46, 48, 49, 51, 53*
Rosie Martin, *110, 111, 114, 115, 117, 119, 126, 129*

Sigrid Wright, *245, 247, 248*

Susan Glisson, *261, 263, 264, 265*

See also leaders, Courage & Renewal Academy for Leaders, *36*

Courage to Lead for Nonprofit Leaders, *65*

Courage to Lead retreats, *98, 145*

'courage to stay', *283*

Courage to Teach retreats, *98*

courage types,
   creative, *167, 169*
   moral,
   social,

Courage Way,
   community ingredient of, *9, 119, 120*

fortifying for the your journey in the, *285, 286*

as guide to leadership, *3, 5*

inner wisdom premise of the, *68*

practice of open, honest questions as part of the, *182*

practicing paradox ingredient of, *9, 10*

reflection ingredient of, *10*

reflective practice ingredient of, *117, 119*

true self ingredient of, *7*

trust ingredient of, *5, 7, 9, 115*

See also Center for Courage & Renewal; specific ingredient,

Courage Work,
   how curiosity is used in, *195, 196*

as individual and communal practice, *119*

Jonathan Zeichner on inner

sanctum built through, *156*
renewal of individuals required for, *170*
Rosie Martin on new understanding through, *115*
the 'third things' used in, *124, 126*
creative courage,
   finding your voice leads to, *167, 169*
curiosity,
   Courage Work use of, *195, 196*
   Einstein on 'holy', *184*
   as valuable asset in society, *195*
   See also open, honest questions,
Curious (Leslie), *195*

D

decision making,
   choosing to risk, *225, 227*

FTE's courage to renew and reinvent itself, *227, 228, 230, 232, 234*
Greg Eaton's story on choosing wisely and, *218, 221, 223*
inner truth used to guide our, *218*
A Rubric for Choosing with Integrity, *236, 238*
trusting the process of choosing wisely, *234, 236*
deep listening,
   applied to performance reviews, *190, 192, 194*
   creating space and opportunities for, *247*
   Jill Boone's defusing of tense situation using, *199, 201*

Mike and Bob's story on not fixing but, *181, 182, 184*
practicing, *181*
See also conversations; no fixing touchstone; silence,
deliberately developmental organizations (DDOs), *195*
Deming, W. Edwards, *272*
Designing Transformative Multicultural Initiatives (Watt), *252, 254*
dialogue,
asking open, honest questions, *14, 22, 24*
Lellene Rector's commitment opening LGBTQ welcome and, *241, 243*

no fixing touchstone guiding, *14, 21*
truth touchstone guiding truthful, *14, 19, 21*
Where I'm From exercise (Welcome Table) to encourage, *261, 263, 264*
wonder touchstone guiding rough, *14, 21, 22*
See also conversations,
Dik, Bryan, *162*
disrespect,
speak your truth without showing others any, *14, 19, 21*
diversity,
Beloved Community's vision of, *274*

creating
trustworthy space
for, *12, 14, 15, 17, 19, 21,
22, 24, 26, 27, 29*
institutions that
truly embrace, *243*
Lellene Rector's
commitment to
LGBTQ inclusivity
and, *241, 243*
Maya Angelou on
beauty of, *248*
welcoming all
sorts of, *251, 252, 254*
Dixie do-Dads
(grandfather's tool
shop), *58, 61, 67, 81*
Duffy, Ryan, *162*

E
Eaton, Greg, *192, 194,
218, 221, 223*
Einstein, Albert, *184*
Embar, Ramya, *137,
138, 141*
emotions,
choosing with
integrity by
noticing your
default, *238*
See also love,
empowerment,
Ed France's
experience of
finding, *79, 81*
how the true self
offers us, *79, 81, 82*
of Kate
Sheppard's
holding the
tension of the
moment, *208, 210*

F
fear couplet (Rumi),
169
finding your voice,
creative courage
founds through,
167, 169
to give voice to
courage, *169, 170*
Habits of the
Heart on, *232*
via negativa or
hard choices for,
163, 165

Fiscus, Lynne,
  application of
  respect to build
  relational trust
  by, *102*
  offered challenge
  of leading a new
  clinic, *84, 85*
  on the 'Parable of
  the Trapeze', *88, 89,*
  91, 93, 95
  personal regard
  for her team
  shown by, *102, 104*
  on relational trust
  in competence of
  her team, *104*
  successful
  Courage-based
  leadership
  applications by,
  85, 88, 89, 91
fixing,
  See no fixing
  touchstone,
fortitude,
  for your Courage
  Way journey
  ahead, *285, 286*

Forum for
Theological
Exploration (FTE),
  Fund for
  Theological
  Education name
  changed to, *234*
  Habits of the
  Heart approach to
  strategic planning
  by, *227, 228, 230, 232, 234*
  Stephen Lewis'
  leadership of, *227*
France, Ed:
  empowered by
  finding his true
  self, *79, 81*
  functional atheism
  suffered by, *79*
  on his
  grandfather's
  tool-lending shop,
  58, 61, 67, 81
  on his 'inner
  space
  exploration', *72*
  on his
  self-determination

vision in community, *67, 68*
on learning self-care and renewal, *65, 67, 68, 77*
on merging Bici Centro with SBBIKE, *63*
Frankl, Viktor, *210*
Franz, Marie-Louise von, *74, 76*
functional atheism shadow, *77, 79*

G
Garrett-Evangelical Theological Seminary, *240, 241, 243*
Glisson, Susan, *261, 263, 264, 265*
'good' leadership, *3*
'Go to the Limits of Your Longing' (Rilke), *39, 41*

H
Habits of the Heart,
1: recognizing that we're all in this together, *228*
2: appreciating the value of otherness, *228*
3: holding tensions in life-giving ways, *230*
4: a sense of personal voice and agency, *232*
5: a capacity to create community, *232, 234*
Hamilton, Hal, *51*
Havel, Václav, *34*
Helsing, Deborah, *29*
Hepburn, Audrey, *129*
Herson, Patrick,
on becoming a doctor, *34, 36*
on building trust, *51, 53*
on leading with compassion, *39, 41, 46, 48*

on regular tending of community, *37, 39, 49*

on ten-meter diving platform metaphor of leadership, *36, 37*

as willing to be vulnerable, *46, 48*

holding space touchstones, *29, 31*

holding tension response,

description and purpose of, *204, 206*

presidential election, *210*

Habits of the Heart on affirming paradox through, *230*

how we can daily engage in, *196*

Jill Boone's open, honest questions and, *199, 201*

Kate Sheppard's story on, *206, 208, 210*

Niki's story on, *212, 213, 216*

Howell, Annie, *29*

I

inclusivity,

Beloved Community's vision of, *274*

creating trustworthy space for, *12, 14, 15, 17, 19, 21, 22, 24, 26, 27, 29*

Lellene Rector's commitment to LGBTQ, *241, 243*

setting the table for genuine welcome and, *261, 263, 264, 265*

welcoming all, *251, 252, 254*

See also welcome touchstone,

inner teacher touchstone,

attend to your own inner teacher, *14*

guiding dialogue and conversations, *24*

inner wisdom,
becoming visible through integrity, *82*
getting to know the self who leaders or, *68, 70*
how to access your true self or, *72, 74*
Popova's 'seismic core of personhood' or, *72*
as underlying premise of the Courage Way, *68*
See also true self,

Inside Out Community Arts, *154*

integrity,
inner work becoming visible through our, *82*
leaders who cultivate, *48*

Parker Palmer on being in presence of, *41*
relational trust lens of, *106, 107*
A Rubric for Choosing with Integrity, *236, 238*

interactions,
relational trust arising from personal, *95, 97, 98*
Sigrid's redesign of CEC space for increased, *245, 247, 248*
third things to find common ground and space for, *124, 126*
touchstones guiding, *15, 17, 19, 21, 22, 24, 26, 27, 29*

interaction touchstones,
commit to and maintain confidentiality, *26, 27*

creating trustworthy space, *15, 17, 19*
guiding dialogue and large-group conversations, *19, 21, 22, 24, 26*
keep growing the seeds planted, *27, 29*
invitation touchstone,
    creating trustworthy space with the, *17, 19*
    extend invitation, not demand, *14*
    Welcome Table process as, *261, 263, 264, 265*
Island magazine, *126*
ITW (Chicago), *266*

J
Jackson, Marcy, *179, 181, 251*
'The Journey' (Oliver), *39, 55*
Jung, Carl, *74*

Just Sentences literacy program, *126*

K
KKania, John, *51*
Kegan, Robert, *29, 195*
King, Martin Luther, Jr., *274*

L
Lahey, Lisa, *29, 195*
Laloux, Frederic, *195, 285*
Lax, Robert, *286, 287*
leaders,
    awakening them with poetry, *53, 55, 57, 58*
    finding your own way, *31, 32*
    holding space for vision and purpose, *29, 31*
    love and patience required of a good, *120*
    touchstones for creating

trustworthy space, *15, 17, 19, 21, 22, 24, 26, 27, 29*
See also courageous leader stories; the self who leads,
leadership,
  'good', *3*
  having capacity to create community, *48, 49, 51*
  Patrick Herson on micro-shift of compassionate, *39, 41, 46, 48*
  reflective, *127*
  the 'what-if' questions of, *5, 7*
  See also courageous leadership,
leading for impact practice, *127*
leading for transformation practice, *127*
leading from within practice, *127*
Leading Together, Building Adult Community in Schools: creation and pilot program of, *98, 100*
school teams creating their own touchstones for, *100*
leading together practice, *127*
leaving,
  courage to leave and still love, *274, 276, 278*
  courage to leave well, *279, 281*
Lederach, John Paul, *167*
Leslie, Ian, *195*
Let Your Life Speak (Palmer), *77, 79, 160*
Lewis, Stephen, Forum for Theological

Exploration (FTE) leadership of, *227*
Habits of the Heart used to frame FTE's strategic planning by, *227, 228, 230, 232, 234*
LGBTQ persons, *241, 243*
life-giving transformation,
  holding tension to bring about, *196, 199, 201, 203, 204, 206, 208, 210, 212, 213, 216*
  Perceval and the Fisher King story on, *217*
  three touchstones as keys to, *216*
listening,
  See deep listening,
Living the Questions (Markova), *184*
love,
  the Center's work as grounded in core value of, *120*
  courage to leave and still, *274, 276, 278*
  and patience required of a good leader, *120*
  Rainer Maria Rilke on the nature of, *120*
  See also emotions,
Lyons, George Ella, *261*

M
Mandela, Nelson, *162*
Markova, Dawna, *184, 225*
Martin, Rich, *115*
Martin, Rosalie 'Rosie',
  chatter Matters charity founded by, *115, 117*
  her personal growth through

reflective practice, *119*
Just Sentences literacy program of, *126*
offering to teach Risdon Prison inmates, *111, 114, 115, 129*
pondering paradox of humility and chutzpah, *114, 115, 117*
on teaching adults to read and reflect, *110, 111*
May, Rollo, *225*
MCD, Inc., *270, 272*
Merton, Thomas, *141, 142, 143, 286*
metaphors,
  See courageous leadership metaphors,
Mike's story,
on asking open, honest questions with Bob, *184, 186, 188, 218*
on gift of listening without fixing, *181, 182*
on open, honest questions in daily life, *188, 190*
Millman, Debbie, *163*
Mission of Charity (India), *138*
Möbius strip,
  choosing with integrity by where you are on the, *238*
  fortifying for your Courage Way journey on the, *285, 286*
  to visualize convergence of courage in the heart, *41, 42, 44, 46, 53, 108, 238*
moral courage,
  examples of individuals with,

N

Niki's story, *212, 213, 216*

no fixing touchstone,
   caution about taking too literally, *218*
   guiding dialogue and largegroup conversations, *21*
   no fixing, saving, advising, or correcting each other, *14*
   See also deep listening; open, honest questions,
Nouwen, Henri J. M., *95*

O

on access to the 'invisibles' through poetry, *57, 58*
   'An Away-Day with the Shadow' by, *76*
O'Donohue, John, *70*

Oliver, Mary,
   'The Journey' by, *39, 55*
   'The Summer Day' by, *55, 152*
Freeway story, *167, 169*
open, honest questions,
   applied to performance reviews, *190, 192, 194*
   Bob and Mike's story on asking, *184, 186, 188, 190, 218*
   building trust with, *194, 195, 196*
   Courage Way practice using, *182*
   guidelines and purpose for using, *177, 179, 181*
   Jill Boone's defusing of tense situation using, *199, 201*
   as leading us to 'holy curiosity', *184*

Mike's use in daily life of, *188, 190*

performance reviews structured with, *190, 192, 194*

practice asking open, honest questions touchstone, *14*

touchstone for guiding dialogue and conversations, *22, 24*

See also curiosity; no fixing touchstone; questions, organizations, deliberately developmental organizations (DDOs), *195*

making skillful transitions and change in, *281, 283*

otherness,

courage to connect depends on valuing, *259*

creating trustworthy space for inclusivity and, *12, 14, 15, 17, 19, 21, 22, 24, 26, 27, 29*

Lellene Rector's commitment to LGBTQ inclusivity and, *241, 243*

richness of our differences and, *259, 261*

welcoming all including, *251, 252, 254*

P

Palmer, Parker J., on being aware of leadership shadow and light, *74*

on 'Circle of Trust', *10*

on community as a gift, *48*

on community to develop sense of true self, *170*

on complicity in world-making as call to leadership, *3*

The Courage to Teach by, *124*

on creative tension-holding to solve problems, *196*

Dave Boyer on influence of, *272*

on debunking myth of organizational power over us, *147*

Diana Chapman Walsh on lessons learned from, *55, 57*

on 'functional atheism' shadow, *77, 79*

Habits of the Heart approach of, *227, 228, 230, 232, 234*

A Hidden Wholeness by, *206, 254, 255*

on his inner teacher, *70*

on how we can support another person's growth, *120*

on importance of reflection, *110*

on inner truth guiding choices, *218*

on learning through reflective practice, *119, 129*

Let Your Life Speak by, *77, 79, 160*

on listening more deeply, *181*

on living with our own inner teacher, *204*

on paradox of faith and doubt, *148*

on the power of vocation, *158*

on presence of integrity, *41*
on richness of our differences, *259, 261*
on selfcare, *129*
on violence as outcome of unresolved suffering, *213*
'what-if ' questions on courage asked by, *5*
on the 'who' question of leadership, *68*
See also Center for Courage & Renewal,
Palmer, Sharon, *55*
Panda, Mukta,
personal and professional struggle of, *129, 132*
reflective practices filling her with hope, *132, 135*

Relaxing, Rejuvenating, Rejoicing in Residency sessions (RRRnR) created by, *135, 137*
ripple effect of renewal efforts of, *137, 138, 141*
'Parable of the Trapeze' (YouTube video), *88, 89, 91, 93, 95*
paradoxes,
choosing with integrity by looking for, *238*
Courage Way and practice of, *9, 10*
expanding leadership by embracing, *167*
of faith and doubt, *148*
Habits of the Heart on holding tension and affirming, *230*

of humility and chutzpah, *114, 115, 117*

of strength and vulnerability, *167*

Parry, Danaan, *88*

Perceval and the Fisher King story, *217*

performance reviews, *190, 192, 194*

personal growth, love as capacity to extend ourselves for another's, *120*

Rosie Martin on her reflective practice and, *119*

personal regard, *102, 104*

Petzet, Heinrich Wiegand, *124*

Philip, Joan, *270, 272*

physical courage, description of,

poetry,

awakening leaders with, *53, 55, 57, 58*

'Go to the Limits of Your Longing' (Rilke), *39, 41*

'The Journey' (Oliver), *39, 55*

'Night Song of the World' (Lax), *286, 287*

'Potbound' (Walsh), *266*

'Relay' (Brown), *281*

'Song of Myself ' (Whitman), *58*

'The Summer Day' (Oliver), *55*

Welcome Table's Where I'm From exercise on writing, *261, 263, 264*

Popova, Maria, *72*

'Potbound' (Walsh), *266*

presence touchstone,

be present as fully as possible, *14*
creating trustworthy space with the, *17*
presidential election (2016), *210*
problem solving,
  creative tension-holding for, *196*
  Jill Boone's open, honest questions and holding tension for, *199, 201*

Q
questions,
  Perceval and the Fisher King story on importance of asking, *217*
  used by Greg Sunter to invite people into conversations, *170, 173, 175, 177*
  'what if', *5, 7*
  Where I'm From exercise (Welcome Table), *261, 263, 264*
  See also open, honest questions,

R
reality,
  Florida Scott-Maxwell on being 'fierce' with, *107*
Rector, Lallene,
  creating a welcome to LGBTQ persons, *241, 243*
  as Garrett-Evangelical Theological Seminary president, *240, 241*
  on limitations of creating a safe space, *257*
reflection,
  Courage Way ingredient of, *10*

Parker Palmer on importance of, *110*
renewal through, *129*
reflective practices, community, *119, 120, 122, 124, 126*
the Courage Way and, *117, 119*
leadership, *127*
Parker Palmer on learning through, *119*
Rosie Martin's personal growth through, *119*
self-awareness by engaging in, *117, 119*
Reinventing Organizations (Laloux), *195*
relational trust, arising from social exchanges, *97, 98*
competence lens of, *104, 106*
importance of, *95, 97*
integrity lens of, *106, 107*
personal regard lens of, *102, 104*
respect lens of, *100, 102*
relational trust framework, Center for Courage & Renewal's research and, *98, 100*
Leading Together: Building Adult Community in Schools program using, *98, 100*
relationships: being in the presence of integrity and investing in, *41*
third things to find common ground and space for, *124, 126*
touchstones creating

trustworthy space for, *15, 17, 19, 21, 22, 24, 26, 27, 29*

Relaxing, Rejuvenating, Rejoicing in Residency sessions (RRRnR) program, *135, 137*

'Relay' (Brown), *281*

renewal,
  Audrey Hepburn on the need for, *129*
  Ed France on learning elf-care and, *65, 67, 68*
  having the courage for, *227, 228, 230, 232, 234*
  Mukta Panda's efforts bringing ripple effect of, *137, 138, 141*
  the ongoing need for, *148, 149*
  reflection used for, *129*

trustworthy space through touchstone of, *14, 27, 29*
  See also self-care, renewal touchstone,
  know that it's possible for the seeds planted here to keep growing, *14*
  protecting trustworthy space through, *27, 29*

resilience,
  arising from self-awareness and true self, *135, 141, 143, 148, 149*
  Courage-based leadership and resilience retreats to build, *85*
  detaching from work to build, *138*
  knowing the self who leads builds, *68*

needing other people in community contributes to, *9*

respect,
 Lellene Rector's commitment to LGBTQ inclusivity and, *241, 243*
 relational trust lens of, *100, 102*
 speak your truth in ways that show others, *14, 19, 21*

Rilke, Rainer Maria, *39, 41, 120, 124*

Risdon Prison, *111, 114, 115, 117, 129*

risk management, *225, 227*

Robèrt, Karl-Henrik, *272*

Rodney King beating verdicts (1992), *152*

Rumi couplet on fear, *169*

S

See also deep listening; dialogue, safe spaces, *257, 259*

Santa Barbara Bicycle Coalition (SBBIKE), *63, 67*

Santa Ynez Bank of Chumash Indians, *212*

Scharmer, Otto, *68, 70*

Schneider, Barbara, *98, 100, 106*

Schön, Donald, *117*

schools,
 Leading Together: Building Adult Community in Schools program in, *98, 100*
 relational trust framework tested in, *98*

Scott-Maxwell, Florida, *107*

self-awareness,
 choosing with integrity with, *236*

engaging in reflection to gain, *117, 119*

resilience arises from care of true self and, *148, 149*

starting with understanding yourself, *82*

self-care,

cultivating community as form of, *49, 51*

distinction between care of true self and, *141, 142, 264*

Ed France on learning renewal and, *65, 67, 68*

Parker Palmer on need for, *129*

possible when a leader speaks the truth, *147*

Susan Glisson's call for, *264*

Vera's creative response to suffering, *143, 145, 147*

See also renewal,

Senge, Peter, *51, 272*

shadow,

of functional atheism, *77, 79*

seen in many '-isms', *76, 77*

of the true self, *74, 76, 77*

Sheppard, Kate, *206, 208, 210, 218, 251*

silence,

challenge of allowing, *182*

Quakers on 'companionable', *58*

touchstone on, *14, 24, 26*

See also deep listening,

silence touchstone, guiding dialogue and conversations, *24, 26* trust and learn from the silence, *14*

Simmons, Greg, *279, 281*

social courage, description of, solitudes, *120, 122*

'Song of Myself' (Whitman), *58*

spaces,
courage exists in the spaces between us, *31*
created for deep listening opportunities, *247*
creating trustworthy, *12, 14, 15, 17, 19, 21, 22, 24, 26, 27, 29*
designed to connect community, *245, 247, 248*
Ed France on his 'inner space exploration', *72*

held for leader vision and purpose, *29, 31*
holding the tension of the moment for opening conversation, *208, 210*
safe versus brave, *257, 259*
third things to find common ground and, *124, 126*
touchstones for holding, *29, 31*

Stafford, William, *70*

Stewart, Dafina-Lazarus, *255*

suffering,
Niki's story on life-giving transformation of, *212, 213, 216*
violence as outcome of unresolved, *213*

'The Summer Day' (Oliver), *55*

Sunter, Greg,
  on building community and trust, *175*
  posing questions on sense of vocation and purpose, *175, 177*
  using questions to invite people into conversation, *170, 173, 175, 177*
Sustainable Equity, *261*

T

The Art and Spirit of Leadership (Brown), *281*
The Circus of the Sun (Lax), *287*
The Courage to Teach (Palmer), *124*
The Fifth Discipline (Senge), *272*
the heart,
  ancient sense and definition of, *41*
  courage as coming from, *46, 48*
  Habits of the Heart, *228, 230, 232, 234*
  leaders willing to be vulnerable, *46, 48*
  the Möbius strip to visualize convergence of courage in, *41, 42, 44, 46, 53, 108, 238, 285, 286*
  See also compassion,
The Moral Imagination (Lederach), *167*
' Night Song of the World' (Lax), *286, 287*
The School Project, *154*
the self who leads,
  getting to know the inner wisdom of, *68, 70, 72*
  Parker Palmer on the 'who' question of, *68*

See also leaders;
true self,
tension,
  holding tension
  response to, 204,
  206, 208, 210
  Jill Boone's
  experience
  defusing, 199, 201
Theory U
(Scharmer), 68, 70
Theresa, Mother, 138
Thinking the
Unthinkable,
  A New Imperative
  for Leadership in
  a Digital Age
  report (2016), 106
'third things',
  description and
  functions of, 124
  finding common
  ground with, 124,
  126
Thurman, Howard,
70, 165, 227
Tippett, Krista, 190
touchstones,

Circle of Trust
facilitated by, 12, 14
  for creating
  trustworthy
  space, 15, 17, 19, 21, 22,
  24, 26, 27, 29
  defining a shared
  commitment to
  hold safe space,
  122
  description of the,
  12, 14
  finding your own
  way through the,
  31, 32
  holding space, 29,
  31
  as keys to
  life-giving
  transformation,
  216
Leading Together
program, 100
Touchstones at a
Glance list of, 14
  for welcoming the
  soul without an
  agenda, 254, 255

See also Center for Courage & Renewal; Circle of Trust; specific touchstone,

transitions,
See change,

true self,
a centered life to honor our, *44*
choosing with integrity with self-awareness of your, *236*
community reflective practice and becoming your, *119, 120*
the courage to stay true to your, *285*
distinction between self-care and care of, *141, 142, 264*
empowerment through the, *79, 81, 82*

learning to access your, *72, 74*
Parker Palmer on community role in developing, *170*
resilience arises from self-awareness and, *148, 149*
the shadow side of the, *74, 76, 77*
trust your wholeness, *82*
understanding that courage comes from our, *7*
See also inner wisdom; the self who leads,

trust,
choosing with integrity by looking for, *236*
courage coming from a deep self-knowledge and, *5*

Courage Way
ingredient of, *5, 7, 9, 115*
creating
relational, *95, 97, 98*
Greg Sunter on
building
community and, *175*
the inner life of, *108*
open, honest
questions used to
build, *194, 195, 196*
'Parable of the
Trapeze'
(YouTube video)
on, *88, 89, 91, 93, 95*
Patrick Herson on
building, *51, 53*
touchstones for
creating
trustworthy
space, *12, 14, 15, 17, 19, 21, 22, 24, 26, 27, 29*
trustworthy space
touchstones,

attend to your
own inner
teacher, *14, 24*
commit to and
maintain
confidentiality, *14, 26, 27*
defining a shared
commitment to
hold safe space, *122*
extend invitation,
not demand, *14, 17, 19*
give and receive
welcome, *14, 15*
know that it's
possible for the
seeds planted
here to keep
growing, *14, 27, 29*
no fixing, saving,
advising, or
correcting each
other, *14, 21*
practice asking
open, honest
questions, *14, 22, 24*

speak your truth in ways that respect other people's truth, *14, 19, 21*

trust and learn from the silence, *14, 24, 26*

when the going gets rough, turn to wonder, *14, 21, 22*

truth,

    care of true self possible when leader speaks the, *147*

    conversations between us creating shared, *31*

    touchstone on speaking and respecting, *14, 21, 22*

truth touchstone, guiding interactions during dialogue, *19, 21*

speak your truth in ways that respect other people's truth, *14*

Tucker, Charles, *261*

Tucker, Estrus, *274, 276, 278*

U

University of Virginia, *98*

V

Vanier, Jean, *84*

Vera's story, *143, 145, 147*

via negativa, *163, 165*

vocation,

    Greg Sunter's posed questions on purpose and, *175, 177*

    listening for the voice of, *158, 160, 162*

    the meaning of calling in, *162, 163*

    via negativa approach to sense of, *163, 165*

    See also work,

vulnerability,
idea of courage coming from, *46, 48*
paradox of strength and, *167*

W

Walsh, Diana Chapman, *55, 57, 266*
Watt, Sherry K., *243, 252, 254*
Welcome Table (Sustainable Equity), *261, 263, 264, 265*
welcome touchstone,
creating trustworthy space with the, *15*
give and receive welcome, *14*
Lellene Rector's commitment to the, *240, 241, 243*
setting the table for genuine welcome, *261, 263, 264, 265*

welcoming all sorts of diversity, *251, 252, 254*
welcoming the soul without an agenda, *254, 255*
See also inclusivity,
'what-if' questions, *5, 7*
Where I'm From exercise (Welcome Table), *261, 263, 264*
whistleblowers,
Whitman, Walt, *58*
William Winter Institute for Racial Reconciliation (University of Mississippi), *261*
wonder touchstone,
as caution about, *218*
guiding dialogue and large-group conversations, *21, 22*

Niki's story on turning suffering into wonder, *212, 213, 216*

when the going gets rough, turn to wonder, *14*

work,

courageous leadership based on bringing your full self to, *158, 160, 162*

holding space for the vision and purpose of, *29, 31*

touchstones creating trustworthy space for, *15, 17, 19, 21, 22, 24, 26, 27, 29*

See also vocation,

workplace,

creating relational trust in the, *95, 97, 98*

leaders who cultivate integrity in the, *48*

whistleblowers in the,

Worline, Monica, *31*

Wright, Sigrid,

creating opportunities for deep listening, *247*

redesigning CEC space to connect community, *245, 247, 248*

Z

Zeichner, Jonathan,

on being called to service work, *162*

challenges providing for his eldest brother, *152*

early life experiences of, *149, 152*

embracing paradox of strength and vulnerability, *167*

110 Freeway story told by, *167, 169*

A Place Called
Home (APCH)
executive director
role by, *154, 156, 167*
on positive
outcomes of
Courage Work,
156, 158
The School
Project and Inside
Out community
Arts started by,
154